"Clint and Penny Bragg are ████████ ██████ ... we have watched them live out their own marriage mission. Every married couple can benefit from the practical tools and unique exercises in this book. If you want to experience God in the midst of your marriage in ways you cannot imagine, then roll up your sleeves and get ready. You will not just read *Your Marriage, God's Mission*—you will live it."

—JOE AND MICHELLE WILLIAMS, founders of The International Center for Reconciling God's Way and authors of *Yes, Your Marriage Can Be Saved*

"Clint and Penny have an amazing story of how God's faithfulness to them has inspired an ongoing mission to minister to marriages, giving their own lives and marriage an incredible depth of direction and purpose. Their new book is a call to all of us to find not only God's design for marriage in general, but also the unique plan for our marriage. This book is wonderfully hands-on and inspiring, giving great insights and ideas of how to discover, engage, prepare, and succeed in fulfilling the rich divine mission and adventure God has in store for every couple willing to walk with Him."

—ROBERT S. PAUL, vice president of Focus on the Family's National Institute of Marriage

"Marriage and mission are two values we hold dear. Every couple needs a field guide like this to gain success in the exciting adventure God has planned for them."

—BILL AND PAM FARREL, authors of 45 books including *Men Are Like Waffles, Women Are Like Spaghetti*

"Whether you'd like to make a good marriage better or you're looking for advice on dealing with the tough issues every couple encounters, *Your Marriage, God's Mission* is the book you need to read. Clint and Penny Bragg offer assessment tools, hard-earned lessons from their own experience and the experiences of others, spiritual direction, and a process for discovering God's mission for your marriage. This book is more than a marriage manual—it's a tool that will lead you to an intimate relationship with the Lord that will positively impact your long-term relationship with your spouse."

—CAROL AND GENE KENT, founders of Speak Up for Hope

# YOUR MARRIAGE
## GOD'S MISSION

# YOUR MARRIAGE

# GOD'S MISSION

### Discovering Your Spiritual Purpose Together

## CLINT *and* PENNY A. BRAGG

Kregel
*Publications*

ISBN 978-0-8254-4427-2

Printed in the United States of America
17  18  19  20  21  22  23  24  25  26  /  5  4  3  2  1

*To Irene Mae Kenna,*
*our beloved "Gramma," who always believed in*
*the mission God set in our hearts and encouraged*
*us to "Go out there and get that second book!"*

*"Have I not commanded you? Be strong and courageous. Do not be afraid; do not be discouraged, for the LORD your God will be with you wherever you go."*

—JOSHUA 1:9

# Contents

*Acknowledgments* . . . . . . . . . . . . . . . . . . . . . . . . . . . . . . . . . . . 11

*Introduction* . . . . . . . . . . . . . . . . . . . . . . . . . . . . . . . . . . . . . . . 13

## Phase I—Induction and Mission Ops

1 Marriage on a Mission . . . . . . . . . . . . . . . . . . . . . . . . . 23

2 Why Marriage Requires a Mission . . . . . . . . . . . . . . . . . 27

3 Taking Stock of What You've Got . . . . . . . . . . . . . . . . 31

4 Your Marriage Mission Statement . . . . . . . . . . . . . . . . 43

## Phase II—Basic Training

5 Weapons Training . . . . . . . . . . . . . . . . . . . . . . . . . . . . . 53

6 Marching in Formation . . . . . . . . . . . . . . . . . . . . . . . . . 67

7 Breaking Down Fear . . . . . . . . . . . . . . . . . . . . . . . . . . . 79

8 Preparing to Possess . . . . . . . . . . . . . . . . . . . . . . . . . . . 89

## Phase III—Planning and Protocols

9 Operational Order . . . . . . . . . . . . . . . . . . . . . . . . . . . . 101

10 Your Marriage Mission Creed . . . . . . . . . . . . . . . . . . . 111

11 Sharing Your Rations . . . . . . . . . . . . . . . . . . . . . . . . . . 121

12 Active Duty . . . . . . . . . . . . . . . . . . . . . . . . . . . . . . . . . . 133

## Phase IV—Hazards and Hostiles

13 Know Your Enemy . . . . . . . . . . . . . . . . . . . . . . . . . . . . 143

14 Sneak Attacks . . . . . . . . . . . . . . . . . . . . . . . . . . . . . . . . 157

15 Incoming! . . . . . . . . . . . . . . . . . . . . . . . . . . . . . . . . . . . 167

16 The Beauty of Battle Scars . . . . . . . . . . . . . . . . . . . . . . 181

## Phase V—Checkpoints and Charges

17  Patrolling Your Borders ......................... 191
18  R and R ........................................ 201
19  Forward, March! ................................ 215

*Appendix A: Resources for Recovery* ......................... 227
*Appendix B: Resources for Recovering from Loss* ............... 229
*Notes* .................................................. 231

# Acknowledgments

From its inception many years ago, *Your Marriage, God's Mission* generated both excitement and angst in us. Our desire was to craft something highly unique to serve as the catalyst for a Godward movement among marriages. But how? Writing this book became a mission in and of itself, which we never could have accomplished alone. Our gratitude runs deep and wide for the many eyes, hearts, and hands that have touched this work in its varying stages of development over the last several years. They include . . .

Our God: You alone are our one desire. We bless You, Father!

Our family: We are grateful for your ongoing love and encouragement.

Our financial supporters: Your faithful giving is unprecedented, and it allows us to stretch our services from state to state and country to country. We are forever thankful.

Our agent: Amanda Luedeke, you were so very worth the wait.

Our manuscript prayer team: Melanie Brookey, Loralee Cambier, Becky Duck, Michele Elizaga, Pam Fitzgerald, Colleen Goncalves, M. A. Harris, and Donna Tinsley, your prayers kept us fueled in every way. Special thanks to our Florida prayer partners, Russell Holloway and Becky Duck, for patiently listening to our concerns about this book from week to week.

Our interviewed couples: Your authenticity and vulnerability in allowing us to put your stories on camera and in written form were paramount to the mission of this book.

Our early proofreaders: Dawn Nassise, Gene O'Dell, and Pam

Fitzgerald, you helped clean up our messy sentences, as did the Word Weavers of Volusia County.

Our thirty-day book launch intercessors: Your powerful prayers sent this book forth with God's blessing.

The Kregel team: Dennis Hillman, you have spoiled us twice now with a spectacular publishing experience. Bless you. Steve Barclift, you are always our pick for managing editor of the year. We heap a wealth of gratitude on Janyre Tromp for overhauling and reshaping the manuscript and on Bob Hartig for refining and tightening our words. We also wish to specifically acknowledge those individuals behind the scenes who helped this book round its final turn: Noelle Pedersen and Katherine Chappell for preparing the marketing campaign and tools for the book's launch. Joel Armstrong for carefully setting each correction into place. Dawn Anderson for previewing the videos and providing valuable feedback. Michelle Reinhold and Lori Alberda for lending us your eyes of wisdom.

# Introduction

The high rate of separation and divorce in our nation and around the world proves that most couples today exist without a coordinated mission. The lack of common purpose makes it easier to throw away a relationship when expectations go unmet, or to exchange it for something, or someone, new.

Some couples believe there is a reason they are together, but they're stuck in a revolving door of careers, church, pressures, parenting, and more. Penny and I have also met couples who believe God has a particular mission for them, but ambiguity and confusion arise when we ask if they know what that mission is. Almost always they say the same thing: "We know we're supposed to do something together as a couple, but we don't know what that looks like."

We ourselves have been in all these scenarios and then some. It took us a long time to realize that our past experiences, as difficult as they were, would eventually lead us to God's mission for our marriage. To properly set the stage for further reading and application so you can move forward, allow us to take you back into our failure at both marriage and finding God's mission for our lives.

Less than two years after we said, "I do," we were done. In some ways, our relationship ended before it—or God's mission for it—ever got off the ground. We had dated for two years before getting engaged. In addition, we went through premarital counseling, took personality tests, and met with our pastor. All the basics of Christianity 101 were exhibited once we married: attending church, praying over meals, and serving others. We thought that believing in God and loving each other were enough to make for a lasting relationship. Wrong.

Although deep down we knew that God had brought us together for a reason, we never stopped to ask Him what that reason was. Instead we made assumptions about what our life was going to look like, what we wanted out of our marriage, and what we were going to go out there and do for God. Unwittingly, we set off on a crash course to make our own hopes and dreams come true. And we crashed.

With one year of marriage under our belts, Penny and I set off on an overseas mission. Our pastor had a connection to missionary work in Papua New Guinea, and we eagerly signed on. However, we were disappointed when our plans for a summer-long mission to New Guinea turned into a two-week trip to Haiti.

"This isn't going to be very challenging," I remember saying to Penny. "Maybe we should hold out for something more . . . adventurous."

When our first morning in Haiti included an infestation of fire ants in our makeshift bed (wooden planks stretched across a cement slab), I realized we'd gotten ourselves into a little more than we expected. Still, we weren't about to wimp out.

I'd spent two tours fighting in Vietnam, so our accommodations didn't jar me that much. In the army, I'd spent many nights sleeping on top of an APC (armored personnel carrier) in the jungle. I was a little worried about Penny and what she might be feeling, but I never asked her about it. After all, we had a mission to accomplish. My military mind-set governed my actions and interactions with her and with everyone else.

Our two main goals were to construct a cement-block building, which would function as both a church and a school, and to share Christ with those living in tiny thatched huts. Being in Haiti reminded me of my time in Nam, and my military training allowed me to emotionally disconnect myself from the immense poverty and sickness we witnessed.

I (Penny) began rethinking overseas missions when the fire ants crawled up our legs that first morning in Haiti. Day two was no better. Our team spent ten hours standing up in the back of a flatbed truck that traveled through the jungle on a narrow, unpaved road. Like buoys in the ocean waves, we bobbed up and down with every bump and pothole. Guards in battle fatigues stopped us several times, pointing loaded rifles in our direction. At each checkpoint I held my breath. I wasn't ready to die!

Eventually we arrived at our worksite and set up camp. At our first meeting there, Clint and I were asked to serve on separate work teams. This unnerved me. I didn't want to be apart from him, but I wasn't comfortable expressing my concern. Clint was assigned to the building crew, and I was sent off into the jungle with the evangelism team. My insides rattled way down deep. While we walked slowly from hut to hut, garnering the strength for what we were about to do, my fears mounted. The farther into the bush we journeyed, the further my gut lodged itself up in my throat.

Walking along the dusty pathway, we approached two women escaping the intense heat by stretching out under the shade of a tiny tree. One of them said she had been robbed in the city, and her husband murdered. She was twenty-three.

As we continued walking, another woman with a sick baby and a severely malnourished toddler rushed out from their hut and begged us for medicine.

"Please help me! My baby is sick," she cried out in Créole. She shoved the baby into my teammate's arms. "Take her with you to America."

Through our interpreter, we discovered that the infant was suffering from worms, diarrhea, congestion, and malnutrition. There was no money for medicine. We prayed for the baby and told the mother we'd try to help. She followed us to the next hut.

I peeked inside. There on the dirt floor was a crippled man curled up in a ball, a bag of bones. The hut was dark and smelly. I was afraid something might happen to me if I went all the way inside. The suffering of these people was more than I could bear. To add to my fear and distress, we were taunted by voodoo bands at night along the roadside. I was *this* close to being over the edge, but I didn't say anything to Clint. To anyone. After all, we were doing great things for God and living out His mission for our marriage.

On our final morning, the whole team gathered together for Bible study, prayer, and worship. As we sat in a circle, a woman suddenly burst from the bushes, ran over to Clint, and climbed on his lap. Before I could think, I jumped up, grabbed the woman, and pulled her off him. She screamed at me in Créole. I couldn't understand a thing she said, but I knew it wasn't good. Clint and I never talked about what happened.

Disillusioned, stunned, and shaken by the suffering I'd witnessed, I found no gauge to measure or process what we'd experienced. Once we got home, there was a strange disconnection between Clint and me—a gap that only widened over time. My faith was slowly being eaten away from the inside; Clint wanted to go on another mission.

Gradually I distanced myself from my responsibilities at church and started hanging out with new friends from college. As Clint and I continued to struggle, my thoughts morphed into drastic decisions. Eight months after our return from Haiti, I packed a few things in a suitcase and walked out our front door. Marriage and mission—aborted.

Clint and I aren't trying to place the blame for our demise on that one overseas mission. We take full responsibility for our marital crash and burn. There were actually many miracles during that trip, and we were grateful to be a part of what God did there. But in the end, we were not just worlds apart; we were in completely different galaxies. As a result, we bottomed out before our second anniversary. Once our divorce was finalized, we turned our backs on each other and walked away.

Eleven years of complete silence passed between us.

When God began reconnecting us in 2002, we were finally able to speak openly about our blowout. Among many other things, we talked about that mission to Haiti and how whatever happened there had sent us into a tailspin. Haiti was the beginning of the end.

In hindsight, we also realized that our problems ran much deeper. That overseas mission just unearthed them. For years the difficulties we endured as children had been stuffed down and glossed over with strong facades. When the unexpected happened in Haiti, we were unprepared for what it triggered. That one trip brought ugly things to the surface, and we didn't know what to do with them.

Perhaps if we'd realized we were two broken people in need of much mending, things would have turned out differently. Instead we were full of pride and blind to our own brokenness. We harped on our unmet needs and each other's shortcomings. While we were convinced that we were ready for God's mission, we were totally unprepared for marriage.

When God miraculously reconciled us, we knew that we had to make some major changes. Instead of focusing on ourselves, we asked God to heal our brokenness and set us on an intentional course to pursue Him as a couple. In the process of doing so, God revealed His mission for our marriage—a mission we *never* saw coming. It's the reason behind this book. Our mission is YOU.

## HOW TO USE THIS BOOK

My (Clint's) induction into the Unites States Army began with a physical exam and a series of assembly-line inoculations. Next I was officially sworn in by oath to defend my country. Once that was complete, the other GIs and I were transported to Travis Air Force Base and, finally, Fort Lewis, Washington, for basic training. Upon arriving, we were stripped of our clothes and given fatigues and the standard military buzz cut. Like well-oiled machines, the drill instructors in command bounced us from one person to another. There was a precise way to do everything.

There is something to be said for that kind of regimented approach. While there isn't a perfect prescription to begin discovering God's mission, we suggest that you start by setting aside one hour each week to read this book together, pray, and discuss the questions at the end of each chapter. For consistency, try your best to meet at the same time, day, and place each week. Think of these meetings like regular mission updates or business briefings from a commanding officer or CEO (God). You wouldn't dream of launching a mission, going into battle, or implementing a business plan without meetings. Why would you approach your marriage any differently?

If you've never tried something like meeting regularly with your spouse, it may take some getting used to. Give yourself time. And realize that Satan will work hard to keep you from meeting consistently. Disagreements will tempt you to skip out on being together. It will take an unwavering commitment from each of you to make this time together a high priority. Your marriage is worth it. God's mission is worth it.

During your weekly meetings, turn off the demands of the day. Set aside the distractions of cell phones and other screens. Taking proactive precautions to alleviate interruptions will help you focus and concentrate on each other. If you have young children, you'll need to make arrangements for their care. But be assured that what you're doing as husband and wife will greatly benefit your kids and create a lasting impact on the future generations of your family.

As in life, some chapters in this book are more involved than others. Don't feel that you have to rush through a reading. You may or may not get through one chapter each week. That's okay. Any worth-while endeavor takes time, effort, and energy.

To enhance your experience, QR codes are embedded throughout the chapters. If you don't have a QR code reader app installed on your smartphone or tablet, we highly recommend that you download one and use it to scan these codes. Each one will link you to videos of other couples on missions from God. (You can also access these videos with a web browser at https://marriageonamission.com /video-journal/.) Our hope is that you'll glean insight and inspiration from their stories.

One final suggestion: keep a notebook or journal to record what God is doing as you meet together each week. (You can each keep your own journal or use one in which both of you write.) For some people, journaling elicits a visceral response. However, reflecting in writing on what God is doing, and responding to what unfolds, is a powerful way to retrace your footprints and derive meaning from your experiences. Try not to overanalyze or edit your thoughts and feelings. Express yourself freely. You'll be amazed at the way your journal becomes not only a running record of your experiences, but also a treasured part of your marriage legacy and a testimony to God's faithfulness.

Consider this book a training manual intended to facilitate an encounter with God as husband and wife. Over the course of reading it, you'll strap on the sandals of Joshua, Nehemiah, Jesus, Paul, and others whose hearts were resolutely set on God and His mission. Our prayer is that in the process of encountering Him in *their* lives, you'll discover God's specific mission for your marriage. Make no mistake, He has one—a mission uniquely yours.

Because some couples may not be accustomed to praying together, we've included a prayer at the end of each chapter. You'll also find discussion questions to help you apply what you've read. Reading the chapter is only a small part of your experience. You'll work out your marriage and mission muscles when you pray together, talk about what you've read, and discuss the questions.

You'll get out of this commitment what you put into it. That being said, hold on. You're setting a course for a unique discovery mission with God where absolutely anything is possible. Are you ready? Good. Let's move forward!

*Phase I*

# INDUCTION AND MISSION OPS

## Chapter 1

# Marriage on a Mission

*If you take missions out of the Bible, you won't*
*have anything left but the covers.*
—NINA GUNTER

The Bible is full of special people sent on specific missions. Moses's mission was to bring the Israelites out of bondage in Egypt. Joshua's mission was to lead God's people into the Promised Land. Rebuilding the ruined city of Jerusalem was the task given to Nehemiah. Esther's mission was to save her people from annihilation. Jesus's mission was to do the will of God the Father. The apostle Paul was charged with spreading the gospel and establishing the early church.

Not only did God choose certain individuals to carry out specific missions, but He also chose couples. In the Old Testament, God revealed His original design for marriage through Adam and Eve. Abraham and Sarah were chosen to give birth to many nations in order to establish God's covenant. In the New Testament, Joseph and Mary's mission was to parent the Savior of the world, Jesus Christ. The charge of spreading the gospel was given to Priscilla and Aquila. All these couples were given a marriage mission: a specific task assigned by God to be carried out together to accomplish His will.

In fact, God has a mission for *every* marriage, including yours. No matter your age, ethnicity, socioeconomic status, life circumstances, or denomination, there is something unique that He wants you to accomplish together over the course of your lives. Whatever God's mission for your marriage includes, it is designed first to honor Him and then to impact others.

The goal of *Your Marriage, God's Mission* is to help you discover God's mission for your marriage and assist you in its development, growth, and ongoing assessment. To do so, we'll share about our own process of discovering God's mission for our marriage as well as that of other couples we've met along the way. You'll also find helpful tools and innovative ideas within these pages, but we promise not to spoon-feed you with prescriptive advice or a set of linear steps. Discovering God's mission for your marriage isn't a program. It's a process. While we often wish we knew both the end result and the means to get there, God isn't like that. Neither is marriage or His mission for it.

However, we do know that discovering and living out God's mission will give your relationship a much greater sense of purpose and meaning. Your marriage, unreservedly set on God's mission, possesses the power to impact families, neighborhoods, churches, communities, and the world! And no one is better suited for the task than you.

Just as no two marriages are alike, God's mission for every marriage is also unique. The processes He uses to guide each couple differ as well. As your marriage grows and your life circumstances change, your mission may also change or morph into something new. Or you may have one solitary mission throughout your entire marriage.

Having said all that, there is a common purpose in every mission: God created marriage as the vehicle by which the gospel is transported throughout all generations. As you experience God together, your earthly mission will begin to reflect that purpose, set forth before time began. "For we are His workmanship, created in Christ Jesus for good works, which God prepared beforehand that we should walk in them" (Eph. 2:10 NKJV).

In these latter days, as we await the return of Jesus Christ, our world is quaking with financial upheaval, tragedy, terrorism, shifting weather patterns, and health epidemics that span the globe. We believe God is giving His people one last opportunity to reach up and grab hold of His heart, His plans, His purposes, and His mission.

This is *your* chance.

Now that you understand a little more about what a marriage mission is, the remaining chapters in this phase will explain why your marriage needs a mission and how to discover yours.

---

## Pray Together

God, there is much more to marriage than we ever imagined. We believe You have a purpose and a mission for us to accomplish as a couple. Help us discover the task You have assigned to our marriage. Open our hearts and minds to hear what You are saying as we begin this process together. Make us sensitive to Your Holy Spirit and give us wisdom to make choices in accordance with Your will. Help us remain faithful and committed to meeting each week, without interruptions. Guard us from allowing other things to take precedence over this time we're setting apart. Our marriage and mission belong to You. In Jesus's name. Amen.

---

## Taking the Next Step

Use these questions as discussion points. You may also wish to record some answers or insights in your journal.

1. When you hear the word *mission*, what images and words come to mind?
2. What do you hope to gain from meeting together each week? Discuss your hopes and expectations as well as your concerns.
3. Choose the day of the week, time, and place you'll meet each week. Identify any possible distractions or interruptions. What will you do to protect this commitment?

## Chapter 2

# Why Marriage Requires a Mission

*Marriage has the power to set the*
*course of your life as a whole.*
—TIMOTHY KELLER, *The Meaning of Marriage*

There are several reasons why the marriage relationship requires a mission. We already know that missions are one of God's primary means to accomplish His will on earth. But the purpose of a marriage mission doesn't stop there. The process of discovering God's mission allows you to encounter Him as a couple. In other words, discovering God's mission for your marriage is also about discovering God. The process is just as important as the final outcome.

Let's use the very first couple recorded in the Bible as a tangible example of this truth. Adam and Eve were designed to be the model of God's marriage covenant, and right at the start of their mission, they had the opportunity to encounter God. The Bible says that Adam and Eve "heard the sound of the LORD God as he was walking in the garden in the cool of the day" (Gen. 3:8). God was literally in their midst! But instead of engaging in that intimate experience together, they gave in to temptation and sin. Unfortunately, we live with the fallout of their choices. But because Christ fulfilled

His mission to save us from all sin, we don't have to live under that penalty.

When you choose to pursue God and His mission together as a main priority in your lives, be assured that God will show up. No matter how long you've been married, what your marriage history has included, or what you're up against right now, engaging in the process of discovering God's mission together will serve as a catalyst for an authentic encounter with Him that will change your marriage forever.

Another reason marriage needs a mission is that it puts you in joint pursuit of common goals. Plenty of things in your daily lives can divide or weaken your relationship, such as keeping up with the rapid pace of your surroundings, responding to the varied needs of family members, overbooking your schedules, or meeting the requirements of demanding jobs. People, addictions, and other pleasurable attractions can act as divisive agents. But a marriage set on God's mission means you're both working toward shared goals, serving God together, and experiencing common events.

Our friends Dan and Pam have discovered that God's mission for their marriage is tutoring at-risk kids. We can think of no better couple to carry out this mission than them, given their personalities and talents. Their common goals are not limited to helping these underachieving children perform better in school. They also seek to demonstrate tenderness and compassion for each child's overall welfare. This includes actively helping the children's families by preparing snacks and donating school supplies. When lives are transformed at the tutoring center, Dan and Pam get to experience that joy together. When needs arise, they strategize in prayer and planning. When troubles surface, they share in the same sorrow. Their mission bonds them more tightly together.

In addition to encountering God and working toward common goals, you get to use your gifts, talents, and abilities for the good of others when your marriage aligns with God's mission. For example, one couple at our church is gifted in coordinating and serving people. They combine those skills and carry out their marriage mission by preparing meals for bereaved family members and friends following each memorial service.

Our friends Charles and Melanie possess musical talents. Their mission? To colead worship and inspire the next generation to use their God-given gifts for His glory. Their talents could have easily led them in different directions or put them in a competition against each other. Instead, they have allowed God to fuse those talents and gifts together for the benefit of others.

Conversely, a marriage without a mission has a high potential of running on parallel tracks: two people married by contract and obligation but living separate lives. This type of relationship lacks focus and is ruled by haphazard behavior, impulsive decision-making, and cyclical offense patterns. Picture two soldiers in the same fighting unit whose lack of coordinated effort results in their fighting against one another. What ensues is "friendly fire": spouses misidentifying each other as enemies who eventually become targets. Instead of operating as a unit the way God intended, such couples end up merely coexisting. Oftentimes the distance between spouses increases over time until what started as two parallel tracks diverge farther apart. These marriages pack the highest potential for crisis, separation, and divorce.[1]

Besides running side by side rather than united, a marriage without a mission fails to take its proper place in God's overarching purpose for all mankind. Think of God's greater purpose as a jigsaw puzzle. Each piece is created to fit perfectly together with other pieces, displaying a larger picture only He can see. Some pieces are tiny; some are bigger. Some pieces are void of color; others are vivid. But every piece is needed to fit together and create the overall picture. Take one piece out of the puzzle and the picture is incomplete.

Marriages were not designed for spouses to operate separately but to be joined together as a symbol of Christ's relationship with believers, exhibiting God's glory for all time. The more couples there are who choose to discover God's mission, the more glorious and extraordinary the final masterpiece will be.

---

## Pray Together

God, although we may not know what Your mission for our marriage is yet, we understand why we need to have one. Help us take the next right step in this process of discovery. Make us aware of the gifts and talents You've given us, and show us how we might use them to serve You and others. We need to work toward common goals, but we want them to align with Your will. We want a marriage that is united, not divided. Help us take our place in Your bigger picture. In Jesus's name. Amen.

---

## Taking the Next Step

Use these questions as discussion points. You may also wish to record some answers or insights in your journal.

1. In your own words, explain one reason why every marriage needs a mission. If you're keeping a journal, write down that reason and place today's date next to your entry.
2. Do you know of a marriage that seems to have accepted an assigned task from God? If so, what is their mission and how are they living it out?
3. What are your spouse's greatest strengths, talents, or abilities? What are yours? Do you have any strengths in common? If so, what are they?

# Chapter 3

# Taking Stock of What You've Got

*There has never been a package like you ever before in history, nor will there ever be again.*
—LAURIE BETH JONES, *The Path*

Marriage missions vary drastically. God's creativity is exhibited and displayed by the wide variety of tasks He assigns to His people. To begin the dialogue and discovery of God's special mission for you, think about the kinds of military missions you're probably familiar with. Each one has its unique purposes, characteristics, and challenges.

- *Search and rescue mission*: Enter into an area of destruction and save lives in peril.
- *Courier/cargo mission*: Retrieve and/or deliver goods or correspondence.
- *Fact-finding mission*: Gather data for a specific purpose.
- *Diplomatic mission*: Participate in matters of government or diplomacy.
- *Recovery mission*: Repair or find something that is lost.
- *Spy mission*: Uncover trade secrets and expose enemy plans.
- *Combat mission*: Fight and conquer an enemy.

- *Convoy/escort mission:* Provide protection for and/or accompany others.
- *Reconnaissance mission:* Obtain information on potential enemies.
- *Discovery mission:* Enter uncharted territory hoping to find something new.
- *Encounter mission:* Interact with a particular being, culture, group, community, or tribe.

While God's mission for your marriage may contain various elements of each of these military missions, its most prominent purpose is far greater than all of them combined. God's mission for you is a *sacred* mission. The word *sacred* means dedicated or set apart as special in some way. Your mission is sacred because no one else's mission will be exactly like yours, and you'll travel on holy ground with God—territory already given to you as part of your inheritance in Christ.

You may not be sure exactly what that means yet. That's okay! Penny and I weren't sure either. All we knew was that God was stirring something in us, and we wanted to discover what that something was. At that point in our lives, we didn't even know God had a special mission designed just for us. However, we made one paramount decision that you have already made: meeting together weekly.

Every Sunday night at seven thirty, we met on our couch, read a verse or passage from the Bible, talked about it, and prayed together. What we were doing seemed simple, but in the long run it would prove revolutionary. What started as just a good idea became the backbone for marital stability and growth. Together we were seeking and encountering God in the quietness of our home, and it was a beautiful thing. Unbeknownst to us at the time, these meetings would also become the means through which we'd discover God's mission.

Weekly Devotion Time, Ron and Doris • 4:20 *minutes*

Once we got a consistent weekly meeting routine down, we decided to read a Christian book together too. One of our most significant experiences occurred when we read Bruce Wilkinson's *The Dream Giver*, a modern-day parable. The book tells the story of Ordinary, a person who leaves everything familiar to pursue his Big Dream. When we reconciled, we both felt God had planted a dream or seed of some sort in our hearts. *The Dream Giver* watered our seed and gave it a ray of sunlight. We began actively dreaming with God. *What if we were able to help other couples in some way? What if God has a special purpose for our marriage that reaches far beyond us? How can we figure out what that purpose is?*

## STEP ONE: IDENTIFY YOUR INTERESTS

Perhaps you have a dream, or maybe just a slight inkling, about your mission as a couple. It could be something like, "A common desire we both share is to help underprivileged children in our neighborhood. Maybe that's part of our mission."

No mission is too great or too small. While your head may be swimming with uncertainties, one thing you can be assured of right now is that God has given you special interests, hobbies, and talents that will contribute to the mission He has for you. Start there.

You may or may not be aware of *all* the abilities God has given you, but you can probably name some personal hobbies and interests. On the following pages you will find an extensive list that combines all these things; look through the list and circle the top ten items you possess to the greatest degree. You may find it helpful to think about the things others have said about you, such as, "You're so good at teaching," or, "You're such an encourager." Once you've circled your

top ten, place a star next to the areas where you think your spouse
excels. (If you think of something that is not on the list, add it.)

Accounting

Administration

Advertising

Analysis

Animals

Apostleship

Architecture

Art/drawing/graphics

Athleticism and
   sports

Automobiles

Bereavement

Bookkeeping

Brainstorming

Celibacy

Charismatic gifts

Childcare

Communication

Conflict resolution

Connecting people/
   ideas

Cooking

Counseling

Crafts

Creativity

Critical thinking

Decision-making

Design

Detail orientation

Discipleship

Editing

Elderly care

Empathy

Encouragement

Evangelism

Faith

Financial planning

Foreign language

Gardening

Giving

Healing

Health/fitness

Helping others

Honesty

Hospitality

Human resources

Humor

Imagination

Initiative

Innovation

Inspiration

Interior design

Interpersonal skills

Intrapersonal skills

Intuition

Keyboarding

Landscaping

Leadership

Learning

Legal work

Listening

Maintenance/routine
   tasks

Management

Marketing/advertising

Martyrdom
   (willingness to face
   persecution for
   your faith or cause)

Math

Mechanics

Mentoring

Mercy

Missions

Music

Nature

Negotiation

Networking

Office work

Organization

Pastoring

Photography

Planning

Prayer

Preaching

Problem-solving

Programming

| | | |
|---|---|---|
| Project management | Serving | Technology |
| Public speaking | Shopping | Transportation |
| Reading | Sign language | Troubleshooting |
| Recruitment | Singing | Videography |
| Refurnishing/ | Social issues | Visualization |
| refurbishing | Social networking | Website development |
| Relaxation | Storytelling | Woodworking |
| Research | Systems management | Worship |
| Sales | Tax preparation | Writing |
| Science | Teaching/training | |

Now that you've circled your top ten special interests, hobbies, and talents, rewrite them in the space below. You may find it helpful to number them in order of importance to you.

_____ _____

_____ _____

_____ _____

_____ _____

_____ _____

If you want to get more specific in discovering your gifts and talents, the Internet furnishes spiritual gifts inventories that are much more detailed and extensive than what we've included here. But for the most part, the exercise you've just completed is enough to begin honing in on the possible services your mission may include.

## STEP TWO: SELECT ACTIONS THAT ATTRACT YOU

Every mission involves action. The longer you live, the more you realize the types of actions that appeal to you and those that don't. Selecting the verbs or action words that best fit your personality is the next step in discovering God's mission for your marriage. Look at the list of action words on the following pages. Circle eight to ten

verbs that most resonate with you. Notice that some of the words
from the previous list also appear here as action words.

| | | | |
|---|---|---|---|
| Activate | Coach | Defend | Enhance |
| Adapt | Collaborate | Define | Enlarge |
| Adjust | Collect | Delegate | Enlist |
| Administer | Combine | Deliver | Ensure |
| Advance | Communicate | Demonstrate | Entertain |
| Advertise | Compare | Design | Establish |
| Advise | Compile | Detect | Estimate |
| Advocate | Compose | Develop | Evaluate |
| Affirm | Compute | Devise | Evangelize |
| Aid | Conceive | Diagnose | Examine |
| Amplify | Conceptualize | Direct | Execute |
| Analyze | Condense | Discover | Expand |
| Arrange | Conduct | Dispense | Expedite |
| Ascend | Conserve | Display | Experiment |
| Assemble | Consolidate | Dissect | Explain |
| Assess | Construct | Distribute | Explore |
| Assist | Consult | Divert | Express |
| Attain | Contribute | Document | Extend |
| Augment | Convert | Draft | Extract |
| Balance | Convey | Earn | Fabricate |
| Boost | Convince | Edit | Facilitate |
| Budget | Coordinate | Educate | Fashion |
| Build | Correspond | Eliminate | Finalize |
| Calculate | Counsel | Embrace | Find |
| Capture | Create | Emphasize | Fix |
| Catalogue | Critique | Employ | Focus |
| Centralize | Cultivate | Encourage | Forecast |
| Clarify | Customize | Enforce | Form |
| Classify | Debug | Engineer | Formulate |

| | | | |
|---|---|---|---|
| Foster | Institute | Merge | Pray |
| Fulfill | Integrate | Mobilize | Predict |
| Furnish | Interact | Modify | Prepare |
| Gain | Interpret | Monitor | Prescribe |
| Gather | Interview | Motivate | Present |
| Generate | Introduce | Navigate | Preside |
| Govern | Invent | Negotiate | Prevent |
| Guide | Inventory | Nurture | Print |
| Handle | Investigate | Observe | Prioritize |
| Heal | Involve | Obtain | Process |
| Help | Issue | Open | Produce |
| Hire | Join | Operate | Program |
| Hone | Journey | Orchestrate | Project |
| Honor | Judge | Order | Promote |
| Host | Keep | Organize | Proofread |
| Hypothesize | Launch | Originate | Propose |
| Identify | Lead | Outline | Protect |
| Illustrate | Learn | Overcome | Prove |
| Imagine | Lecture | Overhaul | Provide |
| Implement | Liberate | Oversee | Publicize |
| Improve | Lift | Participate | Purchase |
| Improvise | Listen | Pass | Qualify |
| Incorporate | Locate | Perform | Question |
| Increase | Log | Persuade | Raise |
| Index | Maintain | Photograph | Rate |
| Influence | Manage | Pilot | Reach |
| Inform | Manipulate | Pinpoint | Realize |
| Initiate | Market | Pioneer | Reason |
| Innovate | Maximize | Place | Rebuild |
| Inspect | Measure | Plan | Receive |
| Inspire | Mediate | Play | Reclaim |
| Install | Memorialize | Praise | Recommend |

| | | | |
|---|---|---|---|
| Reconcile | Revise | Standardize | Transcribe |
| Record | Revitalize | Start | Transform |
| Recruit | Route | Streamline | Translate |
| Redeem | Run | Strengthen | Transmit |
| Reduce | Safeguard | Structure | Travel |
| Refer | Save | Study | Tutor |
| Regulate | Schedule | Suggest | Uncover |
| Rehabilitate | Screen | Summarize | Undertake |
| Relate | Search | Supervise | Unite |
| Release | Secure | Supply | Update |
| Remember | Select | Support | Upgrade |
| Remodel | Sell | Surpass | Use |
| Render | Separate | Surrender | Utilize |
| Renew | Serve | Survey | Validate |
| Reorganize | Shape | Sustain | Venture |
| Repair | Share | Synthesize | Verbalize |
| Replace | Simplify | Systematize | Verify |
| Report | Simulate | Tap | Vitalize |
| Represent | Sketch | Target | Volunteer |
| Rescue | Solve | Teach | Weigh |
| Research | Sort | Terminate | Widen |
| Reshape | Speak | Test | Win |
| Resolve | Spearhead | Tighten | Work |
| Respond | Specialize | Touch | Worship |
| Restore | Specify | Track | Write |
| Retrieve | Sponsor | Trade | |
| Review | Staff | Train | |

Write your top ten action words in the space below in no particular order.

_____          _____

_____          _____

_____          _____

_____          _____

_____          _____

## STEP THREE: AFFIRM YOUR AFFINITIES

The next step in discovering God's mission for your marriage is to affirm the causes, groups, and categories with which you most identify in terms of serving others. Look at the list on the following pages. Circle three or four of the causes, groups, or categories that most interest you.

Abuse

Addiction

Adoption

Agriculture

Alcohol and/or
  substance abuse
  prevention

Animal advocacy

Anti-bullying

Anti-violence

Art

Bereavement/grief

Birth defects

Books

Business

Children's issues

Church life

Construction

Crime/victims' rights

Cultural diversity

Disabilities

Domestic violence

Drunk driving
  awareness

Earth/ecology

Education

Elderly affairs and
  abuse

Energy

Environment

Family issues

Finance

Firearms/gun control

Fire prevention

Foster care

Government

Health/illness

Homelessness

Hospice care

Human trafficking

Hunger

Immigration

Journalism

Justice system

Labor/employment
  issues

Law

Literacy

Management

Marriage

Media

Mental health

Missing children

Missions/evangelism

News

Nonprofit agencies

Nutrition

Orphans

Parks/recreation

Patriotism

Peace

Performing arts

Police lost in duty

| | | |
|---|---|---|
| Politics | Rape and sexual | Technology |
| POW/MIA | assault | Travel |
| Public safety | Real estate | Veterans |
| Publishing | Recycling | Water |
| Pregnancy/ | Sexual addiction | Widows |
| reproduction | Sexual assault | Women's issues |
| Pro-life | Social media | Youth |
| Racial issues | Spirituality/religion | |

In the space below, write the causes, groups, and categories you marked.

_____        _____

_____        _____

Congratulations! You may not realize it yet, but completing these exercises has helped you take your next steps in the process of identifying your marriage mission. In the following chapter, we'll guide you in putting more of the pieces together so you can begin drafting a joint marriage mission statement.

## Pray Together

God, You have uniquely created us as individuals. Your Word says we are wonderfully made. Thank You for the creative ways You've wired us. We understand that our interests, hobbies, and talents play an important part in Your mission. Help us become people of action who are identified with the causes and groups that honor You. As we take these next steps together, we need Your wisdom and insight. Keep us open to Your will and Your changes of direction. Combine our different personalities in such a way that Your mission will be greatly enhanced. In Jesus's name. Amen.

## Taking the Next Step

Use these questions as discussion points. You may also wish to record some answers or insights in your journal.

1. Review the military missions listed on pages 31–32. Which one(s) most intrigues you at this time, and why?
2. In the three different word lists found in this chapter, compare your selections with those of your spouse. List any common choices from each of the three categories:
   - Common interests, hobbies, gifts, talents, and abilities
   - Common action words
   - Common affinity groups
3. What specific insights about yourself, your spouse, and God's mission did you discover from the exercises in this chapter?
4. Are you any further along on your discovery of God's mission? Why or why not?

# Your Marriage Mission Statement

*"Call to me and I will answer you and tell you great*
*and unsearchable things you do not know."*
—JEREMIAH 33:3

One advantage of living in biblical times was that most missions were audibly expressed by God the Father, by an angel, or by Jesus Christ. In some instances, people were also told where to go, what to do, and what to say. Here are some examples.

*Joshua*: "Be strong and courageous, because you will lead these people to inherit the land I swore to their ancestors to give them" (Josh. 1:6).

*Jeremiah*: "Before I formed you in the womb I knew you, before you were born I set you apart; I appointed you as a prophet to the nations" (Jer. 1:5).

*Ezekiel*: "Son of man, I am sending you to the Israelites, to a rebellious nation that has rebelled against me; they and their ancestors have been in revolt against me to this very day. The people to whom I am sending you are obstinate and stubborn. Say to them, 'This is what the Sovereign LORD says'" (Ezek. 2:3–4).

*Joseph*: "After [Joseph] had considered this, an angel of the Lord appeared to him in a dream and said, 'Joseph son of David, do not be afraid to take Mary home as your wife, because what is conceived in her is from the Holy Spirit. She will give birth to a son, and you are to give him the name Jesus, because he will save his people from their sins'" (Matt. 1:20-21).

*The twelve disciples:* "Jesus called his twelve disciples to him and gave them authority to drive out impure spirits and to heal every disease and sickness. . . . These twelve Jesus sent out with the following instructions: 'Do not go among the Gentiles or enter any town of the Samaritans. Go rather to the lost sheep of Israel. As you go, proclaim this message: "The kingdom of heaven has come near." Heal the sick, raise the dead, cleanse those who have leprosy, drive out demons. Freely you have received; freely give'" (Matt. 10:1, 5-8).

Today, God uses the discovery process more often than audible impartation. But you have the Bible as your reference to guide you. In addition, you have the Holy Spirit. There are also several tools in this chapter to assist you in drafting your *marriage mission statement*: a single sentence that clearly conveys your assigned task.

## MISSION REGULATIONS

By studying the missions of others, we've created a list of general characteristics all God's missions had in common. Like military regulations, this list will help govern your mission overall and keep the development of your marriage mission statement on target. Your mission should

- be an assigned task(s) that is in alignment with what the Bible teaches;
- make an impact on at least one other person;
- be articulated in a one-sentence mission statement;
- contain joint goals and purposes;
- be characterized by an action or series of actions you carry out together;

- be agreed upon by the two of you;
- be confirmed by other people of faith you respect, such as your pastor, ministry leaders, or others in authority positions; and
- be flexible and open to change/redirection as needed.

## MISSION IMPACT

When I joined the service, our country was engaged in the Vietnam War. While I may not have known anything about being a soldier, I believed my strengths and interests in operations and mechanics would be put to good use for my country.

That's how it is with you and your marriage mission. Look back at all the choices you made with the word lists in the previous chapter. Your interests and abilities can be of much use to God's kingdom. He'll use whatever you give Him.

To your interests and abilities, add your heartfelt concerns: things you want to see addressed or changed. Your scope of vision for change can be your family, your church, your neighborhood, your community, your state, your country, or the world. What excites you and ignites your passion? What gets you all fired up? What breaks your heart in two? What circumstances have attracted your attention?

Place a check mark by the possibilities below that best describe the need you see in the world.

\_\_\_  Something broken that needs to be mended
\_\_\_  A commodity that is lacking
\_\_\_  An underprivileged or marginalized group of people
\_\_\_  Something that must be stopped or prevented
\_\_\_  A cause that burdens your heart
\_\_\_  A group of people for whom you feel a particular connection
\_\_\_  A passion you want to ignite in others
\_\_\_  Something you can't accomplish alone
\_\_\_  A service you are able to perform

___    Something unique you have to offer
___    A program, class, ministry, or outreach that needs your help
___    A vision or dream you long to fulfill that will impact others

## MISSION IMPARTATION

Some missions are imparted through life-changing experiences. Take Pedro and Tania, for example. After encountering the radical and unconditional love of Christ in their own broken lives, they can do nothing less than share that same love with others who do not have a relationship with Him. Whether they're sitting across the table from someone having coffee or launching out on an overseas mission together, they tell others about God's ability to rescue a reckless life from self-destruction. Their mission is to seek out, serve, and love lost and broken people.

Many missions are born out of a crisis, hardship, or tragedy that crashes into our lives—from something painful. Ron and Doris hit a major crisis in their marriage. At the time they felt alone and desperate for resources that would save them from separation and divorce. Years after doing the hard work of healing and restoration, they realized God's mission for their marriage was to facilitate a class for couples in their church.

Other missions come as a response to a felt need. Tim and Joy were confronted with the needs of the Navajo people in the Southwest. Their mission? To share the gospel of Jesus Christ with the Navajos in a relevant way. They accomplish this by spending time with them, building trust, and sharing truth to empower each person, bringing healing from historical and personal trauma.

Some couples discover that their mission is embedded in what they do for a living. Our friends Dennis and Denise opened a joint business of outdoor landscape and interior design. Their marriage mission is to share God's love with their customers.

We've also known other couples whose missions have come from a vision or dream. In 1985, Gordon and Earlyne had a vision to start a nondenominational Christian radio station to share the gospel over the airwaves. At the time, race relations in their city were immensely strained, and there was much competition between churches and denominations. Their vision gave birth to WAPN Radio 91.5 FM in Holly Hill, Florida, which is still on the air today.

## DRAFTING YOUR MISSION STATEMENT

Important: You don't need to have your mission all figured out by now. Some couples will; many won't. However, once you determine what God's mission for your marriage is in general, you can begin the process of articulating it in a one-sentence statement. Think of it this way: If you only have ten seconds to tell someone what God's mission for your marriage is, what would you say? To help you, here are some examples of concise marriage mission statements.

Our marriage mission is to . . .
* feed free breakfasts to the needy children at our kids' school.
* pray for the sick and visit them in hospitals.
* lead our children and grandchildren to faith in Jesus Christ.
* use our extra bedroom to house college students from other countries.
* repair old bicycles and give them to children in the inner city.
* fund missionary couples.
* open our home after school for neighborhood kids in need of a safe place to do homework and make friends.
* provide handyman services to widows and single mothers.
* pick up leftover bread and pastries from local grocery stores and take them to a local homeless shelter.
* create videos that share the gospel message in creative ways.

Your mission may be making peanut-butter-and-jelly sandwiches for the homeless, boxing Christmas gifts for the poor, or greeting newcomers at church. No matter what the details involve, every mission God assigns has value.

Note that none of the sample marriage mission statements explains exactly how the mission will be carried out. That comes later. However, as you continue meeting individually with God, meeting together each week to read this book, and praying about God's mission, He will reveal the details you need when the time is right.

With much trial and error, Clint and I engaged in the discovery process for over a year before we could figure out God's mission for our marriage and articulate it with a one-sentence statement. Regardless of whether or not you are ready to draft your marriage mission statement, take heart. You are making excellent progress. This is hard work but well worth it. Remember, many lives are at stake. Every great mission is the result of great effort.

God's Mission for Us, Bobby and Jen • *5:47 minutes*

God's Mission for Us, Rob and Panda • *3:12 minutes*

God's Mission for Us, Eugene and Ruth • *6:07 minutes*

## Pray Together

God, thank You for being creative and caring. You have uniquely crafted every detail of our lives and we trust You. Don't let us try to rush this process. Help us hone in on our mission and write a statement that reflects what You want us to accomplish together. Impart Your words and ideas to our minds and hearts. Our desire is to stay fully submitted to Your will as we continue moving forward. Pour out Your anointing on us. In Jesus's name. Amen.

## Taking the Next Step

Use these questions as discussion points. You may also wish to record some answers or insights in your journal.

1. At this point, do you think your marriage mission is being imparted through a life-changing experience, a tragedy/crisis, a felt need, or a dream to make a difference? Explain your answer.
2. Considering the work you've done up to this point, are you ready to begin the process of drafting a one-sentence marriage mission statement? Why or why not? If you are ready, use the selections you made in the previous chapter and your spouse's selections to begin drafting it below or in your journal.
3. What thoughts, feelings, and ideas does the illustration to the right stimulate? How does it relate to what you've read regarding your relationship with each other and moving together toward God's mission?

*Phase II*

# BASIC
# TRAINING

Chapter 5

# Weapons Training

*Praise be to the LORD my Rock, who trains*
*my hands for war, my fingers for battle.*
—PSALM 144:1

When I enlisted in the army, I went through eleven weeks of basic training. The goal was to turn civilians into soldiers and prepare us for our missions. In a similar way, consider the chapters in this phase your boot camp in preparation for carrying out God's assigned task.

During basic training, our platoon was issued both offensive weapons (used to attack or counterattack) and defensive weapons (used to protect ourselves). First and foremost, each soldier was issued an M-14 rifle. This was our main offensive weapon against the enemy.

Our rifles were our best friends. Our drill sergeant taught us how to clean, hold, take apart, put back together, carry, and fire them with accuracy. Among other things, we engaged in daily target practice.

To increase our accuracy, targets were placed in front of us at various distances. I quickly discovered that learning to shoot my rifle on target involved more than just pulling the trigger. I had to learn how to use my rifle in a variety of challenging circumstances. Therefore, my training in marksmanship also included how to shoot from many different physical positions, such as crouched down or lying flat on my stomach. Learning how to fire accurately under stress was part of my drill as well. I also ran for miles with my rifle over my head to increase my physical endurance.

In the same way, a marriage on a mission must learn all the aspects of using the offensive weapons God issues His people. As believers, you've been issued a suit of spiritual armor that includes your main offensive weapon, the sword of the Spirit—the Bible.

## YOUR OFFENSIVE WEAPONS

In the military, one of the goals of basic training is to learn rules, procedures, and routines. One routine paramount to the success of your marriage and mission is personal daily time with God. It is your responsibility and privilege to meet with God each day and learn more about Him and the Bible.

If you are the parent of young children, carving out time alone with God is no doubt a challenge. However, it is also a wonderful opportunity to be creative as to what your time with Him might entail. The same holds true if you are working long hours, caring for an ill or elderly family member, or have other demands on your time. Here are a few creative suggestions to incorporate the Bible into your daily responsibilities.

- Use a Bible-verse coloring book with your care receivers.
- Take a walk and listen to an online audio Bible on your smart-phone.
- Print or copy verses of the Bible onto card-stock paper and read them aloud with your kids. In addition, have them illustrate the verses. Post these verses around the house, or bind them together to create a big book.

- Use a short daily devotional such as *One-Minute Inspirations for Women* by Elizabeth George or *One-Minute Insights for Men* by Jim George.
- Read a children's Bible aloud and let your kids dramatize the stories.
- Purchase or download a children's worship album and listen to it together.
- Listen to an audio Bible in the car as you run errands or commute.

If you're able to carve out some quiet time alone with God each day, and you work best with a specific model to use, then we suggest the following framework as one possible starting point.

## The Bible

- *Read* your Bible or listen to a recording. A good place to start is to read one Psalm and one Proverb each day, or a chapter in one of the Gospels (Matthew, Mark, Luke, and John).
- *Record* a meaningful verse from your daily reading in your notebook or journal. Then write one or two sentences about what that verse means to you and how it applies to your life.
- *Respond* to God by praying about any people or circumstances that concern you. Ask Him for whatever you need. Because you are in the process of discovering God's mission for your marriage, also pray about that.
- *Remember* to thank God for something He has done for you before your quiet time is over. You can do this in prayer or by writing it down in your notebook or journal.

In the military we memorized songs as a part of our basic training marches. Our drill sergeant sang the songs to us one line at a time, and then we sang back exactly what he had sung. Soon we had the songs memorized, and they became part of our marches and drills; they helped us increase our skills and our muscle memory. In the same manner, there are ways to help your brain gain more of God's Word by memorizing Scripture.

For some people, memorization is a difficult task. You may find it helpful to write verses onto separate index cards that you can laminate and carry with you or post in places where you'll see them often. You can also write out a verse repeatedly until you memorize it, or speak it into the voice recorder on your cell phone and play it back until you can say the entire verse without the recording. Another idea is to use your phone's camera to photograph your index card so you have a copy in your photo files. Set your phone alarm to go off once a day, reminding you to recite the verse.

If you're already accustomed to spending time alone with God and you use ideas like the ones in this chapter, we commend you. If *both* of you meet consistently with God each day, you'll notice positive changes in your relationship with Him, each other, and others. You will also be better equipped for your mission. No matter what your assigned task entails, your main weapon is the Word of God. Over the course of your life, you must learn how to carry it, understand how it works, and use it with accuracy. In addition to daily time alone with God, you might consider engaging in a weekly Bible study, listening to online podcasts or sermons, or taking a class to learn more about His Word.

## Prayer

While the army issued me a rifle as my primary weapon, I also learned to fire a machine gun, throw hand grenades and CS gas (commonly known as tear gas), and fire a grenade launcher. These additional weapons gave me more firepower. Similarly, you add to your spiritual artillery when you learn how to pray and how to incorporate prayer into every part of your daily life.

Oddly enough, teaching people how to pray isn't normally covered in most churches. For some reason, it's assumed that people will just figure out how to pray as they go along. Some people say that you learn to pray by praying. Penny and I agree in part. But basic training in prayer should include instruction, modeling, *and* "field training," if you will. Here are some ideas to help you learn how to pray:

- Turn a verse in the Bible into a prayer dialogue with God. For example, you may read, "Cast all your anxiety on him because he cares for you" (1 Peter 5:7), and pray, "God, I am casting all my cares and worries on You because You care for me."
- Pray the psalms. The book of Psalms is a book of prayers. Read the psalms aloud and make them your dialogue with God by personalizing them in your own words. For example, you may read, "Surely he will save you from the fowler's snare and from the deadly pestilence. He will cover you with his feathers, and under his wings you will find refuge; his faithfulness will be your shield and rampart" (Ps. 91:3–4). Your prayer could be something like, "Surely You will save me (or insert your first name) from the enemy and from deadly troubles. You will cover me with Your feathers and under Your wings I (or insert your first name) will be safe. Your faithfulness will be my shield and defense."
- Write down your prayers in a notebook or journal. This will become a running record of your conversations with God and keep your mind from wandering. You can also note answers to prayer in your journal.
- Practice praying aloud with your spouse. One way you can do this is by reciting some of your written prayers out loud with him or her. Another suggestion is to read some of the prayer dialogues aloud that you create from the suggestions in the first bullet point. You can also pray aloud through the Psalms or the prayers at the end of each chapter of this book.

- Learn from others. Listen when people pray aloud. What do you notice and what can you apply to your own prayer life? Ask others how they learned to pray and if they have any suggestions for you. Ask people to pray with you. Ask people to pray for you.
- Dedicate a whiteboard or bulletin board in your house to family prayer requests and answers. Hang it in a prominent place. Writing out prayer requests helps you learn how to pray.
- Read books about prayer.
- Husbands, practice praying with your wife by putting your arm around her and reading a prewritten prayer with her or saying a prayer in your own words.
- Incorporate more prayer into your weekly meetings together. Ask your spouse about his or her individual needs and prayer requests for that week. Your spouse should do the same for you. Pray about these things right then and also during the week as you meet alone with God. When you meet together the following week, report any answers to prayer.

In addition to learning how to pray, you must learn how to integrate prayer into every area of your daily life. This can be done in a variety of ways. Here are some suggestions:

- Pray with your spouse in the morning before you start your day. Ask for God's daily provision, protection, and presence.
- Pray over meals by thanking God for your food.
- Pray with your children, individually and/or as a group.
- Purchase and use a prayer book that contains prewritten prayers inside of it to address various circumstances and needs. There are many prayer books available in the marketplace today, such as Max Lucado's *Pocket Prayers: 40 Simple Prayers That Bring Peace and Rest.*

- Skim through the Bible for the prayers of others, think about how they apply to your circumstances, and pray them aloud.
- Pray before you start your household chores or workday, asking God to help you and bless your efforts.
- Pray over your paycheck, asking God to bless and multiply your finances.
- Pray with your family throughout every room in your house, dedicating each area to God.
- Set up a closet or extra room in your house as a place dedicated to pray.

 Talking About Prayer, Rob and Panda • *4:32 minutes*

 Talking About Prayer, Dennis and Denise • *3:54 minutes*

## Worship

Worship is your third offensive weapon against all enemies. Worship means to give God reverence or adoration. Most people think of worship as something that is only done corporately in a church or group setting. But worship includes much more than that. Worship can be almost anything that pleases God and gives Him praise. Here are some suggestions for increasing the ways you worship God.

- Listen to a worship song during your daily quiet time and when you meet together each week.

- Tune in to your local Christian radio station while driving or working.
- Dance to uplifting music.
- Draw, paint, or create something with your hands.
- Use the Internet to play worship videos from YouTube or various church websites.
- Take a walk while listening to worship music and notice the beauty God has created.
- Set aside one day each week to rest from your normal activities. The Jews refer to this as keeping the Sabbath: a day set apart to abstain from work in order to revere God.
- Learn from others. Ask other people how they worship God more personally outside the walls of their church.

My military unit was only as strong as its weakest member. The same can be said for your marriage. You must spend the time needed to effectively use the Bible, prayer, and worship. You will become an equipped, well-trained, strong, and unified team of two by making your individual time alone with God a nonnegotiable commitment in your marriage. In doing so, you learn how to use your spiritual weapons and how valuable it is to keep them on you at all times.

## YOUR DEFENSIVE WEAPONS

Unlike a military rifle, the Bible, prayer, and worship are both defensive and offensive weapons. All three can be used to defend *and* protect you.

In basic training, I was issued several defensive weapons that included a uniform, steel helmet, steel-soled boots, and a flak jacket. I had to wear these at all times in combat, which included successive days of heat up to 125 degrees as well as monsoon rains.

As soldiers in God's army and on His mission, we have also been given a suit of protective (and offensive) armor (Eph. 6:14–17), which includes these pieces:

- The belt of truth
- The breastplate of righteousness
- The shoes of peace, which is the readiness to deliver the gospel
- The helmet of salvation
- The sword of the Spirit, which is the Word of God
- The shield of faith

Let's inspect each piece of armor as it relates to your marriage mission.

## The Belt of Truth

The belt of truth keeps your marriage mission on God's terms and based on His truths, not the enemy's lies or the world's ways. Your mission should be measured or assessed with the Bible (more on assessment in chapter 18). Is your marriage mission fully aligned with God's truth?

## The Breastplate of Righteousness

The breastplate of righteousness is like a flak jacket. It guards your heart, the heart of your marriage, and the core of God's mission. Righteousness means being honest, humble, and fair. Is every aspect of your life, your marriage, and your mission operating in complete honesty, humility, and fairness with all people?

## The Shoes of Peace

The boots issued in basic training were designed to carry a soldier over all types of terrain (jungle, desert, mountain, and swampland, to name a few) and protect his or her feet. The shoes you've been issued on God's mission are meant to carry His peace and the peace of the gospel message wherever you go. Do you bring God's peace and the gospel of peace to others through your mission? Are you a peacemaker when you walk through different types of spiritual and relational terrain?

## The Helmet of Salvation

A military helmet is made of material that can stop a bullet from penetrating a soldier's skull. Similarly, the helmet of salvation protects your mind with the truth of your belief in Jesus Christ as the Son of God and your personal Savior. Nothing can penetrate your salvation. Nothing. The helmet of salvation protects the battlefield in your mind. Does your marriage mission guard your salvation and then share that salvation with others?

## The Sword of the Spirit

The Bible tells us that the sword of the Spirit is the Word of God. As stated earlier, the Bible is both a defensive and an offensive weapon. Is your marriage mission based on the Bible in all its interactions, regulations, attitudes, behaviors, operations, goals, and outcomes?

## The Shield of Faith

Faith means that you are completely sure God will keep His promises, no matter what. Your shield of faith protects you from doubt and discouragement. Your shield of faith wards off incoming enemy rounds. In what ways does your marriage mission require you to exercise faith?

Not until I was out on my first mission in Vietnam did I truly understand the importance of each defensive and offensive weapon. In the jungle, I quickly learned that each one served a specific purpose. In one way or another over time, I would need every weapon.

Not carrying them or wearing them was inconceivable; they were a matter of life and death.

## LEARNING THE LINGO

In basic training, I had to learn a whole new language of military vocabulary. Everything had an acronym, and at first I felt illiterate when orders were barked by the drill sergeant. I also had to learn the International Civil Aviation Organization alphabet for two-way radio communication, with each letter represented by a word, such as A-Alfa, B-Bravo, C-Charlie. It was all so foreign, but drill after drill and experience after experience immersed me in this new lingo until I understood it and could use it fluently.

In a similar way, to function on God's mission, you must develop *spiritual language or literacy*: understanding and using the spiritual language of God's Word, communicating with the Holy Spirit, discerning what His voice sounds like, and learning how to interpret what He is saying. Your intimate relationship with God develops and deepens your spiritual literacy, creating a stronger marital unit. Everything in your marriage and God's mission must be erected from the foundation of a relationship with Jesus Christ. But here's the catch: spiritual literacy is the very thing missing from most marriages today, and that lack is tearing our world in two. Most people have a problem connecting their spiritual life to the fractured state of their marriage. But when both spouses are firmly committed to nurturing their individual relationships with God, the Holy Spirit creates a sacred space around your marriage, speaking a spiritual language you both understand.

Having said that, consider the close of this chapter as a shameless plea to launch you into a deeper relationship with God. Hunger for God more than you hunger for God's mission. Penny and I earnestly pray that by the time we part ways at the end of this book, you will

have given Him more access to your hearts than ever before. That's
what makes all the difference.

Seeking God Together, Larry and Carrie • *3:02 minutes*

## Pray Together

God, thank You for not sending us out on a mission ill equipped or
unarmed. We want to participate in Your training regime so that we
can be strong and fit soldiers in Your army. Teach us how to use the
Bible, prayer, and worship as both offensive and defensive weapons.
We desire to establish consistent routines and procedures in our
daily relationship with You and each other. But we need Your power
to make that happen, especially in light of the many demands on
our time each day. Clothe us with Your spiritual armor. Make us
into a spiritually literate couple. In Jesus's name. Amen.

## Taking the Next Step

Use these questions as discussion points. You may also wish to record some answers or insights in your journal.

1. Have you ever participated in a short- or long-term training program? If so, what was the goal of that training?
2. Place a check mark next to the spiritual disciplines you engage
   in during your time alone with God, and list any others you use.
   Put a star next to the ones you are familiar with, and circle the
   ones you want to learn more about. If you aren't currently meeting with God, what will it take to make that happen?

    \_\_\_ Reading the Bible
    \_\_\_ Memorizing verses
    \_\_\_ Praying
    \_\_\_ Journaling
    \_\_\_ Worshipping
    \_\_\_ Studying the Bible (more than simply reading it)
    \_\_\_ Reading Christian books

3. Discuss any areas of struggle in your time alone with God each day. What are your biggest distractions? Brainstorm ways to eliminate them (or perhaps incorporate them).

4. In light of the chapter you've just read, what do you think this verse means: "Everyone who competes in the games goes into strict training. They do it to get a crown that will not last, but we do it to get a crown that will last forever" (1 Cor. 9:25)?

## Chapter 6

# Marching in Formation

*Coming together is a beginning; keeping together
is progress; working together is success.*
—EDWARD EVERETT HALE

In ancient times, powerful empires possessed fighting troops. Those political powers needed an orderly way to move their troops from one place to another. The idea was that without some type of structured drill formation, soldiers would get lost in battle or end up with another unit instead of the one in which they were trained.

Still today, moving troops involves order and precision: a standardized twenty-four-inch step performed at a cadence of one hundred to one hundred twenty steps per minute. Each soldier must learn to perfectly perform these movements. Then and only then can the unit move together on command. I can still hear our drill sergeant hollering, "Your left, right, left!" as our unit performed drills each day. Soon marching in formation became second nature to me and the other men in my platoon.

Because God's missions always involve movement (physical and spiritual actions), you must learn how to move together as one unit with your spouse. The apostle Paul said it like this in Romans 15:5–6: "May the God who gives endurance and encouragement give you the *same* attitude of mind toward each other that Christ Jesus had, so that with *one* mind and *one* voice you may glorify the God and Father of our Lord Jesus Christ" (italics added).

## CHAIN OF COMMAND

In basic training I reported to my drill instructor. He reported to the master sergeant, who in turn reported to a lieutenant or captain. While your marriage is not bound to the same chain of command as that of a military unit, you are required to follow God's chain of command for marriage. Like a commanding officer, God directs you with His Word and the Holy Spirit, and you are to follow Him as one synchronized unit.

According to the Bible, your marital chain of command is that the husband is the head of the wife just as Christ is the head of the church (Eph. 5:21–33). For our purposes, we will state it more simply: the husband should act as the spiritual leader for his wife, and the wife is expected to follow her husband's lead. Some wives just groaned and some husbands tensed up for several possible reasons.

1. *Wives, you are often disappointed because your husband isn't a spiritual leader and doesn't want to be.* Unfortunately, this is very common. Part of the problem may be that your husband doesn't even know what a spiritual leader is, or his perception of one is something he doesn't feel he can live up to. Hence the tension: you want him to be something he isn't while he, rather than risking failure, does nothing.

For those of you in this scenario, we know it's frustrating and heart-wrenching. But remember, God will hold your husband responsible for his actions, and He will hold you responsible for yours. Your husband needs your respect and your prayers. Although this is a challenging problem, it is not impossible to overcome.

Another reason he may not be spiritually leading you is because, deep down, he knows you know more about spiritual things than he does. What should you do? Change what you can change in yourself. This may be hard to hear, but part of the problem may be that your expectations are too high for where he's at spiritually. Even though he may not lead as well as you'd like, verbally affirm the good things he does. Be willing to surrender your control. Maybe you're afraid he'll mess things up, and maybe he will at times. Extend grace. Help him be the best leader he can be by being a gracious, supportive follower.

2. *Husbands, maybe you want to be the spiritual leader, but you don't know how to lead.* Be encouraged: you can learn! As a child, I (Clint) had no spiritual model in the home. When Penny and I were married the first time, I used an authoritarian approach to lead her. That didn't go over well at all. When we remarried each other, I prayed that God would show me how to be a spiritual leader; I asked Him to change me and teach me what I didn't know. He wasted no time. I became a student of what a godly marriage should look like through reading the Bible and other Christian books. It took some initiative, but I also talked to other men about how to lead and carefully observed their interactions with their wives.

What if your wife won't follow your lead? There are several possible reasons why. She may be flat-out disobedient. That's something only God can change, but the more you show her unconditional love, the likelier she is to respond favorably. Pray for her. Remember, God will hold her responsible for her actions and you for yours.

Perhaps your wife does not yet trust your lead. That was the case for me (Penny). I'd grown accustomed to living as an independent woman, and I needed Clint to earn my trust. He did so by admitting he had to learn how to lead in a new way and by demonstrating his willingness to be teachable.

Your wife may never have had a model of a godly wife in her life, or she may think that following means being wimpy, void of strength or opinion. Pray that God will bring into her life a woman who can be a good influence. Build relationships with other couples from whom both of you can learn. Sometimes it helps simply to ask your wife why she isn't following your lead. You might be surprised by her answer.

3. *Husbands and wives, what if your spouse isn't a Christian and is living contrary to everything the Bible teaches?* There is no simple answer, but there is hope. Though a marriage in this position is probably not ready to receive or carry out a mission from God, stranger things have happened. Look in the Bible. You'll find many examples, such as Hosea, where only one spouse was following God. The Bible says that a wife of faith can, through her behavior, win over her husband to God (1 Peter 3:1). This is by no means an easy task, and it requires counsel, prayer, and study. As you unconditionally love your spouse, stick to your beliefs and values. You need God's strength and comfort. If you're feeling alone in your marriage, there are ideas and resources available. For starters, here are a few suggestions:

- Tell another Christian you can trust and ask him or her to pray regularly with you about your marriage. (This person should not be someone of the opposite sex.)
- Access Christian books that address husbands and wives who are married to an unbelieving spouse.
- Pray for your spouse's salvation daily.
- Focus on strengthening your individual relationship with God.
- Ask God for the ways in which He wants to use your marriage to change your own heart.

Talking About Leading and Following, Pedro and Tania •
*7:28 minutes*

## BECOMING A SPIRITUAL FOLLOWER

Being married is the hardest thing I (Penny) have ever done. As a child I was independent and self-reliant, a born leader. Those tendencies followed me into adulthood and came in quite handy while pursuing my educational career. Following someone else's lead wasn't even in my realm of thought. I had no model of what a godly wife looked like, and I cringed every time I heard the word *submission*. My broken past included relationships with dominating, authoritative men. As I got older, I subconsciously vowed never again to live under any man's thumb.

The morning God urged Clint to start praying with me every day before work, I was shocked at the way he took the lead, and he was surprised that I was willing to follow. It took some practice, but once he put his arm around me and we started praying together daily, I felt our marriage getting stronger. To this day we do not leave the house without praying together. As of this writing, we have started well over five thousand days in prayer as husband and wife.

During my time alone with God each morning, I begged Him to change my heart and show me how to be a wife, even though I had no idea what that really meant. God had to file down a lot of rough edges and change my entire perception of what it meant to follow Clint's lead. My journal was a sounding board for all my questions about being the kind of wife God wanted me to be. It still is! Over time I learned to take every need and concern first to my heavenly husband, Jesus Christ, and then to my earthly husband, Clint.

Becoming a Spiritual Follower, Eugene and Ruth •
*4:23 minutes*

## GETTING BACK IN STEP

In basic training I encountered strict emotional and physical consequences for being out of step during marching drills. Extra push-ups, KP duty, and cleaning the latrine were customary. Sometimes our entire unit got punished because one man stepped out of line. In the long run, those consequences were for the good of the fight.

When we step outside of God's will in speech, action, or reaction, there are consequences, some more obvious than others. Some consequences may be immediate and others may take place down the line. If you say or do something contrary to God's ways, His Holy Spirit will relay that information to your heart. But you have to learn to listen and pay attention.

In a marriage, God's plan is that both spouses stay in the center of His will. Part of how you do this is by speaking and acting in ways that align with the Bible. Your consistent, daily time with God is one way you stay in step with what He wants. God's will encompasses His entire plan for mankind along with every minute detail of your lives together.

Sometimes your marriage gets out of step because you've stepped on each other verbally or emotionally. Men, listen up: because you are designed to be the spiritual leader of your home, take the initiative to get your marriage back in step. Call for a cease-fire. This may consist of things like confessing, apologizing first, making amends, and giving or extending forgiveness. Sometimes the process of getting back in step will involve only you, your spouse, and God; other times it may involve your kids or other people around you. There is no greater attribute a man can have than being the first to admit he is wrong, out of line, and sorry for his part in the breakdown. (More information on confession will be covered in chapter 14.)

Talking About Forgiveness, Ron and Doris • *2:38 minutes*

## TRUST TRAINING

In the army, I had to learn to trust my commanding officers and the other guys in my unit. Those trusting relationships developed in basic training became a matter of life and death once I hit the combat zone. I had to trust the person giving orders and follow the lead of the officers in charge. I had to trust that the guys in my unit would follow directions and that we'd protect each other from harm.

In your relationship with your spouse, a lack of trust can kill your marriage and God's mission for it. So how do you engage in this process of trust training?

At least five different kinds of trust affect your lives together: relational trust, sexual/physical trust, financial trust, professional trust, and spiritual trust. Trust broken in any of these areas prior to or during your marriage will impact your relationship with your spouse. For example, in my (Penny's) early twenties, I had an extremely harmful experience with a pastor, and my spiritual and physical trust were shattered. As a result, my distrust of men in spiritual authority escalated.

Shortly after, I met and married Clint. When our marriage hit the point of crisis, I refused to accept counsel from our church's pastor because of my past experience. Clint and I didn't understand that the pain of broken trust from my past was negatively impacting the ways we interacted with each other and those around us.

Sometimes our spouse will unwittingly do or say something that triggers a difficult memory or broken place in us, and our self-protective emotional responses go on high alert. We may become angry, fearful, upset, and defensive because something in the present has touched a painful wound from the past. As a result, our leading and following in the marital chain of command get stuck.

Take Rob and Donna, for example. Rob's parents divorced when he was five due to his father's affair. Rob lived with his mother, who constantly micromanaged his life. His trust with his father was broken, and his mother constantly butted into his life, so he didn't trust her either. When he left home, he looked forward to making his own independent choices and taking control of his life. Years later, he married Donna.

Donna grew up in a chaotic home that included outbursts of rage from her dad. When she got married, she subconsciously vowed to maintain a safe and orderly environment. Each time she asked Rob to clean up a mess he made or complete a chore around the house, he got angry and verbally fired off at her the way her father did when she was young. As a result, Donna shut down. The combination of Rob's desire to have independence in his life and Donna's need for a controlled environment set them on a chronic collision course, and they couldn't figure out why. Unbeknownst to either of them, their actions triggered broken trust from the past. For years this one problem kept them out of step with each other.

## EXPOSING BROKEN TRUST

Because broken trust affects leading and following in marriage, you must be willing to discuss with your spouse areas of broken trust from your past. It's not easy to do, but it's necessary. Whether during your childhood, adolescence, or adulthood, trust can get broken in various ways. Look at the following list and circle any of the ten trust breakers that have impacted your personal life. Keep in mind that you're engaging in this exercise for the purpose of fact finding (learning more about yourself and your spouse), not fault finding (blaming yourself, your spouse, or someone else).

1. Lies/dishonesty
2. Abuse (emotional, physical, sexual, spiritual, financial)
3. Broken promises
4. Separation and divorce (especially of your own parents)
5. Infidelity
6. Illness (yours or someone else's)
7. Death of a loved one
8. Losses (people, places, things)
9. Violent crimes/traumatic events
10. Other misconduct and sin

Trust can be broken by various people or groups. Look at the list below and circle any who have broken your trust in the past.

Spouse
Parents
Other relatives or family members
Friends
Leaders (including teachers, caregivers, pastors)
Colleagues
Classmates

Revealing areas of your life where trust got broken requires extreme vulnerability, sensitivity, tenderness, and compassion from both of you. Moreover, if your spouse is one who broke your trust, you'll have an added layer of difficulty to work through. However, all this can be accomplished using some of the tools in this chapter.

Exposing broken trust is risky and uncomfortable. You are revealing scars you may have never shown to anyone else. And your spouse's wounds are just as painful and difficult for him or her to disclose to you. If necessary, ask a mentor or counselor to assist you with the process of disclosure and help you pursue healing from past wounds that still need care. And remember: what you and your spouse share with each other is confidential.

 Talking About Brokenness, Bobby and Jen • *3:51 minutes*

## BUILDING MUTUAL TRUST

Besides exposing places of broken trust, you also need to deepen your trust in one another. Mutual trust is an important component of leading and following in marriage, and it doesn't just happen. It takes work on the part of both spouses.

The list below contains ideas for building and rebuilding trust in your marriage. Discuss them with your spouse; find out which ideas most appeal to him or her and which do not. Trust issues are different for each person, and what builds trust for you may be different from what builds trust for your spouse.

- Notice the little things that are important to your spouse—those things that make him or her tick.
- Encourage your spouse's hopes and dreams.
- Acknowledge his or her efforts and goals achieved.
- Ask about your spouse's interests.
- Encourage your spouse's hobbies.
- Call just to say hello.
- Send your spouse an unexpected card, email, or text.
- Make yourself available to listen to your spouse's problems, not fix them.
- Find a common hobby to share together.
- Complete a service project together.
- Go out for a coffee date.
- Go for a walk together. Talk and pray as you walk.

- Find a song to call your own.
- Arrange a date with God together.
- Leave a love note in an unexpected place.
- Give verbal confirmation and affirmation.
- Exchange a love note or gratitude journal. Write your thoughts in the journal and pass it to your spouse. He or she may respond to what you've written and perhaps write something as well before passing it back to you.
- Use your ears more than your mouth.

Trust training in your marriage is like exchanging a fragile gift back and forth between the two of you. If you owned a rare and valuable crystal vase, for example, you would carefully hold it or hand it to your spouse so it wouldn't get dropped or broken. You wouldn't throw it around the house or take it out in public. Instead, you would keep your precious vase in a safe and protected place.

The ideas for trust training contained in this chapter must continue throughout your marriage. As you actively engage in the practice of exposing broken trust and building mutual trust, the flow of leading and following will become a more natural and normal part of your relationship—one that will enhance your ability to move toward God's mission for your marriage as a cohesive unit.

---

## Pray Together

God, You are our commander. We want to learn to follow Your lead and move together as one unit on this mission. Sensitize our hearts to hear Your voice and know the leading of the Holy Spirit. We desire to move according to Your commands. Teach us how to lead and follow using Your guidelines for marriage, not ours. Give us the models and examples we need. May we always be willing to admit our wrongdoings, apologize to each other, and ask forgiveness. Show us more effective ways to sort through our differences and disagreements. Help us to be intentional about exposing broken trust and building trust in our marriage. Keep us both in step with You. In Jesus's name. Amen.

---

## Taking the Next Step

Use these questions as discussion points. You may also wish to record some answers or insights in your journal.

1.  Husbands, what is the hardest part about being a spiritual leader? Wives, what is the hardest part about being a spiritual follower?
2.  Do you find it easier to ask someone for forgiveness or to extend forgiveness to someone who asks you for it? Explain your answer.
3.  Explain the relationship between moving a troop by marching in time and moving forward as a unit on God's mission for your marriage.
4.  Husbands, tell your wife one thing she does well in her relationship with God and with you. Wives, do the same for your husband.
5.  Why is it difficult to disclose vulnerable experiences from the past? Does fear, shame, or the risk of rejection keep you from sharing? Explain your answer.

## Chapter 7

# Breaking Down Fear

*[Anxiety] does not empty tomorrow, brother, of its*
*sorrows; . . . it empties today of its strength.*
—ALEXANDER MACLAREN, "Anxious Care"

Before my unit left basic training and deployed to Vietnam, our drill sergeant set about developing our mental toughness and breaking down all our fears. His tactics were not pretty. But if we let fear fragment our minds and cloud our ability to think clearly, we would not survive our mission out in the field. Basic training was designed to shatter all our previous belief systems and fears, and to build us back up in alignment with one another, ready for battle.

Whatever the details your marriage and mission include, it will probably involve a battle with fear, if it hasn't already. The enemy won't give up a square inch of land without a fight. In the service, we had an oft-repeated saying: "Knowledge replaces fear." If you increase your knowledge about a given situation, you have a better chance of conquering the fear associated with it.

In this chapter, we'll look first at various reasons you may experience fear on God's mission, and then at how to combat what you're afraid of.

## FEAR OF LEAVING FAMILIAR COMFORTS

Sometimes you'll experience fear with regard to God's mission because you're leaving familiar terrain (literal or symbolic). God asked Abram to pick up and leave Ur. He asked the disciples to leave their fish-catching jobs behind. And for Penny and me, He asked us to move across the country. In 2007, we sold our house in California and moved to Florida. Leaving family and friends was the absolute last thing Penny wanted to do. Even though she knew God had led us to let go of everything familiar and we told Him we would do so, she was afraid of leaving her friends and family. She cried all the way across the United States, filled with anxiety over leaving behind every person and place she had known for over forty years. Still, we knew it was God's will.

## FEAR OF FAILURE

In basic training I had to pass certain tests, including a grueling twenty-six–mile forced march. If I did not meet army standards, I'd be "recycled"—forced to start basic training over from the very beginning. Fear of failure hung over my head every single day of those eleven weeks.

Depending on your personalities and circumstances, a fear of failing God or others may kick in as you keep moving toward God's mission. But don't let that discourage you. Even the bravest warriors in the Bible experienced this type of fear.

Take Joshua, for example. If you remember, God gave him a mission to lead the Israelites into the Promised Land. Moses had been given the same charge; however, God's people, due to their disobedience, wandered through the wilderness for forty years, and Moses never led them into Canaan. Now it was Joshua's turn. Would he fail like Moses did? Perhaps. Was he fearful? You bet. But God gave him this encouragement:

Be strong and courageous, because you will lead these people to inherit the land I swore to their ancestors to give them.

Be strong and very courageous. Be careful to obey all the law my servant Moses gave you; do not turn from it to the right or to the left, that you may be successful wherever you go. Keep this Book of the Law always on your lips; meditate on it day and night, so that you may be careful to do everything written in it. Then you will be prosperous and successful. Have I not commanded you? Be strong and courageous. Do not be afraid; do not be discouraged, for the LORD your God will be with you wherever you go. (Josh. 1:6–9)

Because the words "Be strong and courageous" appear three times in that passage, you know there was fear in the camp. God had given Israel three hundred thousand square miles of land to possess, a large portion of which was inhabited by fierce enemy nations. Accepting God's gift meant entering a battleground and risking failure. No one likes the prospect of going to war and losing.

When Steve and Michelle opened a Christian coffeehouse in the midst of a downward economy, they were concerned about becoming another failed small business statistic in their city. "There are so many small businesses going under in the downtown area," Steve said at the time, "but Michelle and I still sense that opening the coffee shop will give people a place to gather and connect. What we're doing feels risky and we are afraid we won't succeed. However, we're moving ahead unless God slams the door shut. I'd rather fail by trying than fail not having tried at all."

Steve and Michelle embraced the risk and God responded to their big step of faith. Their coffeehouse became a bustling hub for fellowship, worship, and unique Christian events.

## FEAR OF DISPLEASING IMPORTANT PEOPLE

Getting a case of nerves before a new endeavor is normal. But concern, criticism, or contradiction from important people in your life—those you love and respect the most—can dramatically increase your anxiety.

Before Nehemiah began his mission to repair the walls of Jerusalem, he experienced a terrible fear of displeasing his boss, the king of Persia. The Bible says that in the king's presence, Nehemiah was "very much afraid" (Neh. 2:2). Other translations say "dreadfully afraid" and "very frightened."

Clint and I felt tremendously edgy before embarking on a mission to Greece and Israel in 2011—alone, without the security of a group tour. Actually, the whole trip seemed like an outrageous idea: to simulate what a couple experiences as they set out to discover God's mission for their marriage. The notion was crazy enough, but then came the added anxiety of a major political eruption in the Middle East just days before our departure. Family members and friends sought to change our minds about going: "This is too dangerous. It's just not safe over there, and we think you should cancel the trip. Why take an unnecessary risk?"

It was difficult to move forward, knowing that we were going directly against the wishes of those we cared for the most. Their intentions were true and good. They were concerned for our lives.

"It's so hard to know we're causing an uproar with our friends and family," I confessed to Clint. "What do *you* think we should do?"

"I can't explain it," he said, "but I know we're supposed to go."

Regardless of what others said, I felt the same way. What we were about to do was becoming increasingly unpopular, but we knew deep down that we had to go. And go we did. Even though we experienced some scary moments overseas, those two weeks remain as a hallmark of our marriage. Every single day of that trip was paramount to exponentially growing our faith, and the trip gave us a unique perspective on God's mission that we wouldn't have had if we'd stayed home.

## FEAR OF DANGER OR INJURY

Some of God's missions involve danger (emotional, physical, relational, or financial). Your body's natural response to danger is God given; it's often called a fight-or-flight response. In my eleven weeks of basic training, I was placed in scenarios to incite the fear of danger in order to develop skills for combat. For example, one day I was mismatched in a pugil-stick (long sticks with pads on each end) fight against a comrade much bigger than me. Afraid of getting hurt, my adrenaline kicked in, and I fought as hard as I could, emerging the unscathed victor.

Like my mismatched pugil-stick fight, God's missions are sometimes physically dangerous. When we first met Dan and Heli, they shared their history of serving God together, including some of the dangers they faced early on. One incident that occurred while they were raising up a new church in Colombia has stuck with us over the years, especially when we've been tempted to cave in to the fear of physical harm. Heli described it like this:

> One Sunday morning before church, I decided to take our daughter out for a walk while Dan stayed home with our infant son. As we walked down the street, a man suddenly appeared and demanded money from me. He pulled up his shirt sleeve to reveal a crowbar and threatened, "If you scream, I'll hit you." All I had of value were my wedding rings, and I was not about to give them up. In fear for our lives, I began repeating the command, "In Jesus's name, leave us alone!" As quickly as the thief had appeared, he disappeared from my sight, visibly shaken. I ran home and cried on Dan's shoulder, grateful for the Lord's power and protection.

Although God's mission for their marriage included the fear of physical danger, Dan and Heli did not shrink back from the task God assigned to them. Instead they forged ahead, knowing that their lives were in God's hands and He would continue to protect them. "We do not belong to those who shrink back and are destroyed, but to those who have faith and are saved" (Heb. 10:39).

## COMBATING EVERY FEAR

You may feel a bit edgy right now as to how God's plans will play out. You want to surrender and hightail it out before the battle heats up. That is normal. But we've learned something significant about all fear: it can either paralyze you or mobilize you. Paralysis happens when you focus on anything or anyone other than God. Mobilization happens when you honestly acknowledge your concerns and anchor yourselves to God's unfailing promises. You can eliminate or, at the very least, learn to combat fear and anxiety with the spiritual weapons you've been issued. God has already given you what you need to push back all forms of fear and pull ahead as people of action. The Bible says, "God has not given us a spirit of fear and timidity, but of power, love, and self-discipline" (2 Tim. 1:7 NLT).

However, you are human, and it can be tempting to ignore or deny your fears rather than face them. But stuffing your fears will only make them more victorious over you in the long run. Instead, using the Word and writing out a prayer to combat your fear is a tangible way to seek God as a couple and gain victory over your anxieties. Here's a six-step outline of the process to apply to any type of fear you experience on God's mission. We've also written a sample prayer to illustrate this idea.

1. Confess the fear to each other. Try to figure out where it came from and seek to understand it. Ask the Holy Spirit to shed His light on the fear. This process may take some time.

2. Find a Bible verse or passage to write into a prayer dialogue (see page 57). This allows you to claim the truth and power of God's Word over your fear.

3. Whether the fear belongs to just one or both of you, write a prayer *together* against it. Take turns contributing ideas, words, and sentences to form a prayer that expresses both of your hearts. As you write, include the Bible verse you selected in step two. You're thus praying God's promises back to Him together and advancing against the fear as a unit.

4. After you write down the prayer, make copies of it to post in several places (home, office, mirror, car, journal, Bible, and so forth) as a reminder to pray it regularly, with believing hearts.

5. Keep praying, asking, and seeking God. Remember, as stated earlier, His timelines and processes are just as important as His outcomes, especially when it comes to changes in your hearts, feelings, attitudes, and actions.

6. Throughout the process, give thanks for all the ways God answers you. Thank Him as He helps you overcome fear and gives you victory. Observe the ways God works, and praise Him for new thoughts and behavior patterns.

## Sample Prayer

Heavenly Father, we confess our fear of _____. Your Word says, "Such love has no fear, because perfect love expels all fear. If we are afraid, it is for fear of punishment, and this shows that we have not fully experienced his perfect love" (1 John 4:18 NLT). We claim this verse together. Reveal the real root of our fears and worries, and shed Your holy, healing light upon them. May we experience Your perfect love and freedom as we seek You and advance forward. Obliterate every fear with Your power and love. Mobilize us into action! In Jesus's name. Amen.

Fears can keep you from following through on your commitments to God. Praying together is your admission that you need His help. Much more will take place through your written prayers than you will understand at the time you pray them.

In *Prayers of a God Chaser*, Tommy Tenney writes, "God has made His commitment and kept His promises. When He asks you to make a commitment, He stands ready to help you overcome all fear and obstacles to make and keep your commitment to Him. He made provision for our tendency to fail, fall, and falter—it is called *grace!*" Tenney advises, "Mention the doubts you feel concerning your own ability to keep your promise, and express your faith in His ability to keep you, carry you, and lift you higher day after day."[2]

It's okay to admit your fears. In fact, it's vital to confess them to God, whose love can dispel every anxiety. When you surrender your worries to God, you give Him permission to work on your behalf.

Like excess baggage, fear and worry are cumbersome and will weigh you down. Kept in the dark, fear can erect a roadblock. Even though every mission includes fear of the unknown, be assured that as you seek God, He will calm your fears, fight your enemies, crash through your roadblocks, and provide exactly what you need to take that one next, right step on His mission. Confessed to God, any baggage from the past or fear of the future becomes something He can use to help you instead of something that will hinder your mission.

Fighting Our Fears, Bobby and Jen • *6:03 minutes*

Fighting Our Fears, Rob and Panda • *4:12 minutes*

## Pray Together

God, we don't want fear or anxiety to hinder us from pursuing You and discovering all You have in store for us. Use our worries and concerns to mobilize us into action. Keep us walking in the center of Your will and increase our thirst to seek You first each day. We surrender our fears to You: fear of _____ (name the fears). As we journey onward, give us wisdom and guidance through the Holy Spirit. Whenever we're tempted to count the cost along the way, remind us to focus on Your worth. Now is the time to pursue You and fearlessly grab hold of Your purposes. In Jesus's name. Amen.

## Taking the Next Step

Use these questions as discussion points. You may also wish to record some answers or insights in your journal.

1. Are you nervous about any aspect of discovering God's mission for your marriage? Explain your answer. It's normal for spouses to differ in their concerns and fears. This isn't a time to analyze or invalidate your spouse's feelings. It's a time to be real with each other and with God.
2. Compose a prayer together to release your fear(s) based on the outline and sample provided on page 85.

Chapter 8

# Preparing to Possess

*[God] will not send us out on any journey*
*for which He does not equip us well.*
—ALEXANDER MACLAREN, "Shod for the Road"

In the sixth chapter of Joshua, we read that Joshua and his fighting men came face-to-face with their first opportunity for conquest. Before them stood the walled city of Jericho, shut up tightly in readiness for battle. But before Joshua's soldiers could set out on their mission, God required them to perform an odd act of preparation.

All the men born during Israel's wilderness wandering had not yet been circumcised. Circumcision was a critical part of the covenant between God and Abraham (Gen. 17:9–14), yet for years the rite had been neglected. Now, in obedience to God, Joshua made sure it was observed. Circumcision signified the Israelite warriors' sonship to God the Father and bound them in service to Him.

The men stayed in the camp until they were healed (Josh. 5:8). Still, you've got to wonder about the timing. Why inflict physical weakness in the face of such an important battle? Perhaps it was because sometimes people must be weakened—whether emotionally, physically, or spiritually—in order to be strengthened supernaturally. And sometimes God, in order to prepare us for a challenge that only He knows is coming, asks us to do things that don't make a lick of sense.

While God's people likely saw the conquest of Jericho as a matter of strategy, God knew that victory depended on their obedience. Their forefathers did not possess a good track record when it came to following orders. Would this new generation obey His commands?

The Israelites were obedient this time around, and they conquered Jericho as a result. But what lay in store wasn't as easy. They were in for some brutality and bloodshed. So is every marriage on God's mission. It's messy out there. Satan is dead-set on doing whatever he can to see marriages and missions aborted. He has some carefully crafted tactics to get you to quit, and he will attack your marriage in one, some, or all of the following seven key sectors.

## THE SEVEN MARRIAGE SECTORS

### Spiritual
Growth in your faith and spiritual life as individuals, as a couple, and as a family is vital for your overall marital health. While this sector may include serving at your church, service is not a substitute for seeking God. The enemy will try to disrupt your time alone with God and your weekly meetings together. He may seek to turn your time into rote legalism, lacking the fire of faith. Or a hardship may lead you to question God's sovereignty: "If God is so good, why would He allow this terrible trouble to hit our family?" Satan seeks to attack your faith at every turn; he wants you to succumb to doubt and dismay.

### Relational
This sector of your marriage includes all the people in your immediate and extended family as well as the relationships you have outside the home, such as those at church, school, and work. The enemy wants you to be self-seeking, self-serving, and self-gratifying. Where he can create division, bitterness, and unforgiveness, he will. Conflict

is one of his go-to tactics, and unresolved or chronic conflict will suck the life right out of your most important relationships.

## Financial
Anything having to do with money management—investments, budgets, savings, expenses, taxes—makes up your financial sector. Satan wants to keep you in debt, lure you into false security, cause you to worry, and fix your eyes on the world's economy.

## Health
Whatever falls within the area of physical and emotional health, wellness, and fitness is a target for the enemy. He wants you to engage in activities that will harm and hinder your body, and to treat it as an idol for his pleasure, not as a temple for God. Satan wants to ravage your body with sickness and your mind with addiction.

## Professional
This sector involves your career, whether inside or outside the home. The enemy wants you to step on others in order to advance in your job. He wants you to lead with authoritarianism and engage in dishonest business practices. He loves it when your work becomes the highest priority in your life.

## Home
The place where you live is vitally important to your marital well-being. The home sector includes improvements, repairs, and providing protection for your family and your belongings. The enemy wants your home to be chaotic and cluttered with the things of the world. In his eyes, more is better.

## Big Dreams
This sector includes any dreams, ideas, and goals you may have. Satan wants to sabotage your God-given dreams and keep you

living in chronic discouragement, doubt, and defeat. The last thing he wants you to believe is that God longs to fulfill and bless your dreams.

Learning how to effectively conquer every enemy you'll face on God's mission is so important that we've devoted several chapters to it in the "Hazards and Hostiles" part of this book. For now, we will refer again to Joshua to offer a few basic suggestions to aid in your victory.

## REAFFIRM YOUR FAITH

Besides having the men circumcised, Joshua led his people in one other act of obedience: celebrating the Passover prior to entering into battle. God's people hadn't observed Passover since they were with Moses at Mt. Sinai, one year after leaving Egypt (Num. 9:1–5). Celebrating Passover reminded the Israelites that God had rolled back the reproach of their bondage in Egypt, setting His people free to enter the Promised Land.

> "Obey these instructions as a lasting ordinance for you and your descendants. When you enter the land that the LORD will give you as he promised, observe this ceremony. And when your children ask you, 'What does this ceremony mean to you?' then tell them, 'It is the Passover sacrifice to the LORD, who passed over the houses of the Israelites in Egypt and spared our homes when he struck down the Egyptians.'" Then the people bowed down and worshiped. The Israelites did just what the LORD commanded Moses and Aaron. (Exod. 12:24–28)

Reinstituting circumcision and Passover in accordance with God's laws was instrumental in the Israelites' preparation both to do battle and to take ownership of the Promised Land. Renewing their covenant vows strengthened their allegiance to God psychologically and spiritually. These exercises of obedience were vital for full possession of their inheritance.

Because Satan wants nothing less than for you to give up before your mission is complete, you are wise to unite your heart to God's heart through prayer, devotion, discipline, and action. Sometimes Clint and I reaffirm our commitment to God by fasting from meals, spending extra time alone with Him, or taking Communion in the privacy of our home.

Creating a mission scrapbook is one way to reaffirm your faith in God and what He can accomplish. This visual journal can be as simple as gluing photographs into a blank notebook and writing down a few bullet points about what each photo represents. Cutting out positive pictures and phrases from magazines is also energizing to your faith. Consider dividing your scrapbook into seven sections, one for each of the seven marriage sectors described earlier in this chapter.

Here's another idea: place a pad of paper next to an empty jar or jug in your home. Then each time God does something significant, write it down and place the slip of paper in the jar. Over time, take out the slips and recount the things God has done. Increase your faith by increasing the size of the jar and getting a bigger pad of paper.

## EXPECT COMBAT

Every victory requires a battle. When I enlisted in the service, I knew I was entering a war zone. I expected attack. Joshua knew there would be battles involved in his mission too.

Don't let any attack throw you off your mission. Understand that warfare against you indicates you're a threat to the enemy. When God gives His people experiences that feel good, like miracles, revelations, provisions, and victories, then we're content, even ecstatic. But when there's a battle, everything in us wants to recoil and retreat.

The same was true for the nation of Israel. God's people were given three hundred thousand square miles of land as their inheritance to possess—a tremendous blessing. God's Word says, "Your territory will extend from the desert to Lebanon, and from the great river, the Euphrates—all the Hittite country—to the Mediterranean Sea in the west" (Josh. 1:4). But it wouldn't come passively; Israel would have to fight to obtain what was promised to them.

Forewarned is forearmed. When you're confronted with Satan's full arsenal, remember this one thing: you're headed in the right direction. Spiritually lock and load against every enemy. Know ahead of time that doors will close, but others will open. Critics will rear up, but cheerleaders will show up. Problems will pop up, but provision will spring forth. Don't quit. Don't give up. Instead, unite, pray, and march onward. Your mission is not in vain. The Amplified Bible says it this way:

> Be sober [well balanced and self-disciplined], be alert *and* cautious at all times. That enemy of yours, the devil, prowls around like a roaring lion [fiercely hungry], seeking someone to devour. But resist him, be firm in *your* faith [against his attack—rooted, established, immovable], knowing that the same experiences of suffering are being experienced by your brothers and sisters throughout the world. [You do not suffer alone.] After you have suffered for a little while, the God of all grace [who imparts His blessing and favor], who called you to His *own* eternal glory in Christ, will Himself complete, confirm, strengthen, and establish you [making you what you ought to be]. To Him be dominion (power, authority, sovereignty) forever and ever. Amen. (1 Peter 5:8–11)

## DON'T TURN BACK

After the Israelites left Egypt and things grew difficult, they wanted to return to their old lives. They were so desperate to go back that they imagined a much better picture than the reality of their harsh enslavement under Pharaoh.

> As Pharaoh approached, the Israelites looked up, and there were the Egyptians, marching after them. They were terrified and cried out to the LORD. They said to Moses, "Was it because there were no graves in Egypt that you brought us to the desert to die? What have you done to us by bringing us out of Egypt? Didn't we say to you in Egypt, 'Leave us alone; let us serve the Egyptians'? It would have been better for us to serve the Egyptians than to die in the desert!" (Exod. 14:10–12)

Disappointment, fear, grief, and panic make people paint skewed pictures. Turning back wasn't an option for the Israelites, but it was a huge temptation.

The consequences of sin may not be what tempt you to do an about-face, as with the Israelites. But someone or something will make you want to take a U-turn at some point along the way. Some difficulty, loss, financial crisis, broken relationship, fearful event, or maybe a combination of all those things will tug hard on your heart. You'll want to cling to the safety and security of what is familiar. And to add another layer of challenge, your spouse may not be tempted to turn back when you are. That was certainly true for us.

As the reality of living away from friends and family set in during those first six months of our new life in Florida, I (Penny) subconsciously painted pictures of our old life in California and conjured up mental scenarios to get us back home. Like the Israelites, I longed to return to the comfort and stability of what we once had before we gave God permission to send us wherever He wanted. I was tempted to turn away from the very thing I'd so passionately asked of God.

All the while, Clint was completely content (more like overjoyed) to be in Florida. The very thing we'd been praying for was now causing division between us. This was a dimension of God's mission we didn't anticipate. We'd have to learn to let God use our different feelings to create an even greater dependence on Him and to blend our differences. But how?

By staying the course. By uniting and using all your spiritual weapons *together*.

Since we had grown accustomed to sitting together on the couch every Sunday night, we had a dedicated time and place to put our new differences out on the table. I said, "I'm grateful for the beautiful home God has given us, but I really miss my friends and family. I never realized how isolated we'd be. Normally I like being a loner, but everything here just feels so . . . foreign."

Although Clint wasn't feeling the same way, he did his best to listen to me with compassion and pray for me. We reviewed why we had moved, and we celebrated the victories God had given us in the past. Clint never fully understood my fear or sorrow, but he knew it was important to validate my feelings. Clint's compassion made me want to validate his own feelings of joy. Through honest conversations about our differences, God allowed us to cross into new terrain together instead of drifting apart.

When your spouse shares his or her fears and struggles, be a nonjudgmental sounding board. Your spouse needs your encouragement more than your opinions; truly *hear* what he or she says rather than just listening. This intimate level of exchange doesn't come naturally. It takes a lot of practice. Be patient with yourselves and each other as you learn to interact at this level.

Satan can slaughter any couple through a lack of communication, preparation, and defense. He wants you to be reactive, not proactive. So keep your spiritual weapons in your hands at all times. Planning against imminent danger will prepare you to overcome it. The next several chapters give you some additional protocols to follow when things heat up on the front lines.

---

## Pray Together

Gracious God, we understand that oftentimes You weaken us and make us even more dependent upon You. Some of the things You do don't make sense to us, but they happen for our good and the good of Your kingdom. Give us boldness to continue advancing as we face people and circumstances set against the different sectors of our marriage. In Your strength we unite and utilize our spiritual weapons of warfare. Remind us to employ Your Word, prayer, and worship as defenses against every enemy. We partner together in unity for Your glory; may we rise up against the real enemy, not each other. Prepare us to fully possess all that we've inherited as Your son and daughter. In Jesus's name. Amen.

---

## Taking the Next Step

Use these questions as discussion points. You may also wish to record some answers or insights in your journal.

1. Identifying the nature of your opponent is sometimes half the battle. Take time to identify assaults against each of the seven marriage sectors mentioned in this chapter: spiritual, relational, financial, health, professional, home, and big dreams.
2. Which spiritual weapons are you wielding to combat attacks?
3. Discuss a time when you were tempted to turn back to your comfort zone.

4. Access a copy of the song "Painting Pictures of Egypt" by Sara Groves (from the album *Conversations*) from iTunes or another reputable online music source. Print out a copy of the lyrics at www.christianlyricsonline.com or another Christian lyric website. Listen to the song together and discuss it. Several prompts are listed below:

- The lyrics I resonated with most were _____ because _____.
- Some questions I want to ask God are _____.
- I feel most tempted to turn back when _____.
- I can relate to this song because _____.
- I would recommend this song to _____ because _____.

*Phase III*

# PLANNING AND PROTOCOLS

# Chapter 9

# Operational Order

*Sitting down, Jesus called the Twelve and said,
"Anyone who wants to be first must be the
very last, and the servant of all."*
—MARK 9:35

The chapters in this phase of *Your Marriage, God's Mission* have to do with establishing and understanding, to the best of your ability, the plans and protocols God will use to guide you. For our purposes, the word *protocol* refers to the procedures, or system of "rules," governing your mission affairs. We would never presume to perfectly follow or understand all of God's plans; however, Penny and I offer a set of general biblical principles we have learned over time.

In the military, there's an order to everything and for everything. My dad used to say, "Son, there's your way, there's my way, and there's the navy way." Dad had been on active duty with the US Navy during World War II, but I didn't really understand what he meant until I myself enlisted in the service (in my case, the army).

What I didn't understand in basic training made a lot of sense once I was dropped into the rice paddies of Vietnam. My training would now be put to the test. While I had an overall mission to serve my country as a military policeman, that mission consisted of separate missions such as escorting supply vehicles and pulling security for rigs that broke down. Every mission was carried out according to operational orders (OPORDs). OPORDs always followed the chain of command and were the most efficient way to get information across all lines.

Every OPORD followed the same basic framework:

1. Situation—the specific circumstance you're dealing with in terms of both the enemy and your unit
2. Mission—the who, what, when, where, and why of the mission
3. Execution—how what needs to be done will get done: operations/scheme/task/purpose
4. Sustainment—supplies, materials, personnel, transportation
5. Command and control—the succession of commands, signals, passwords, and so on

When I first heard an OPORD given by a commanding officer, it was fast, confusing, and hard to follow. But by practicing good listening techniques and note-taking skills, I mastered the OPORDs so what needed to happen happened with precise execution and success.

There are OPORDs for your marriage and God's mission for it, based on the Bible and the very creative ways God works. As with a military OPORD, there is often some confusion when you're first learning the ways of God. His commands (laws and principles in the Bible) can be hard to follow when you don't totally understand them. Compared to the operating order of the world today, God's ways stand out as counterintuitive, countercultural, and counter-just-about-everything-else.

## GOD'S WAYS ARE UPSIDE DOWN

From the beginning of the Old Testament to the end of the New, God inverts the normal or natural order of things. The word *invert* means to reverse in position, order, direction, or relationship. Simply stated, inverting something means turning it upside down. No one illustrates this concept more radically than Jesus. Look at His teachings in the following passages:

> The greatest among you will be your servant. For those who exalt themselves will be humbled, and those who humble themselves will be exalted. (Matt. 23:11–12)

> For you know the grace of our Lord Jesus Christ, that though he was rich, yet for your sake he became poor, so that you through his poverty might become rich. (2 Cor. 8:9)

> For whoever wants to save their life will lose it, but whoever loses their life for me will find it. (Matt. 16:25)

These verses have one thing in common: Jesus flipped the wisdom of the world on its ear. His OPORDs were not at all what anyone expected as they awaited the coming Messiah. Clint and I refer to this upside-down OPORD as God's Law of Inversion. The key concept to catch is that inversion is a reversal or turning upside down of the natural order. How does that apply to a marriage on God's mission? Through the indwelling power of the Holy Spirit, you can invert a course of action or an attitude from the *natural* order to God's *supernatural* order. Here are just three extraordinary examples from the Bible to further illustrate this point.

## Abraham

At one hundred years old, Abraham is finally given his promised son, Isaac, through whom all nations would come. His response? Out of obedience, Abraham voluntarily binds his son—and his hopes—to the altar and raises the knife of sacrifice. *Abraham chooses obedience over objection.* From Abraham's one inverted action, God's promise of nations coming from Abraham springs forth and is fulfilled (Gen. 22).

## David

After being hunted down by King Saul and forced to dwell in caves, David finally winds up with his pursuer at the end of his spear. David's response? He voluntarily sets Saul free. *He chooses release over retribution* (1 Sam. 24). From that one inverted action, David is blessed by Saul to "do great things and surely triumph" (1 Sam. 26:25). David would eventually replace Saul as king, and through his lineage, the King of Kings would come (Matt. 1).

## Stephen

When the members of the Sanhedrin drag Stephen away to be stoned for his testimony, *he chooses to forgive instead of fight*: "Lord, do not hold this sin against them" (Acts 7:60).

Throughout the Bible, you can trace the favorable fallout of voluntary inversion from generation to generation. As a Christian, you are a product of the inverse choices of those who went before you. Receive that deeply into your spirit. You are here because others before you chose sacrifice over security, humility over honor, and obedience over opportunism.

Inversion is not a measure of morality or martyrdom. It's a matter of love. One voluntary act of inversion is like dropping a pebble into a pond. The power of God breaks the surface of the spiritual atmosphere, and concentric circles immediately spread, ever widening and rippling outward to impact generations and nations for His kingdom. Your children, grandchildren, nieces, nephews, and the generations that follow will live favorably in the fallout of your inverse choices. May they be carried along by the spiritual tsunamis set in motion by your Christlike attitudes and actions today, making mighty waves of their own for tomorrow.

Take a moment to look at a passage from the life of Jesus quoted earlier: "The greatest among you will be your servant. For those who exalt themselves will be humbled, and those who humble themselves will be exalted" (Matt. 23:11–12). Jesus's words rattled the cages of the cultural norm. His life embraced God's Law of Inversion in every way: Jesus came from heaven to earth incarnated as a babe. He touched the untouchable, the lame, and the leper. He entered Jerusalem riding on a smelly donkey instead of in a ritzy chariot. He stooped to wash the dirty feet of His disciples. Finally, He voluntarily took our punishment upon His back. *Jesus Christ chose pardon over payback.*

You will march in step with God when you set a course of making voluntary inverse choices regarding your interactions, behaviors, and attitudes on His mission. But it's not easy. During Paul's mission to spread the gospel and establish the early church, the apostle almost came unglued as he illustrated the dizzying difficulty of behaving inversely:

> We know that the law is spiritual; but I am unspiritual, sold as a slave to sin. I do not understand what I do. For what I want to do I do not do, but what I hate I do. And if I do what I do not want to do, I agree that the law is good. As it is, it is no longer I myself who do it, but it is sin living in me. For I know that good itself does not dwell in me, that is, in my sinful nature. For I have the desire to do what is good, but I cannot carry it out. For I do not do the good I want to do, but the evil I do not want to do—this I keep on doing. Now if I do what I do not want to do, it is no longer I who do it, but it is sin living in me that does it. (Rom. 7:14–20)

## WALKING OUT YOUR FAITH

God's Law of Inversion will always have something to do with walking out your faith in Jesus Christ through your voluntary inverse actions, attitudes, and behaviors. But what does all that really mean? What does it look like each day? It depends on your marriage, your mission, and your circumstances, but here is a general grid.

For each of the seven marriage sectors discussed in the previous chapter, we'll give you a quick synopsis followed by a biblical example and a real-life example of everyday inversion. For the biblical example, we'll use Nehemiah, whom we first met in chapter 1. His mission was to restore the city of Jerusalem after its destruction by the Babylonians. For our real-life example, we'll use Alan and Ann, a couple Clint and I recently met through our church.

### Spiritual

Seek God instead of settling for spiritual lethargy. Stay faithful to your commitment of meeting with God every day, regardless of competing demands.

- Nehemiah mourns, fasts, and prays before beginning his work on the walls of the city (Neh. 1:4).
- Alan and Ann commit to engaging in deeper prayer and journaling to discover God's mission. They set up their journal as a running record of their questions and God's answers during this season of seeking Him with greater intent.

### Relational

Choose sacrifice over selfishness. Be the first to apologize and ask for forgiveness. Let someone else go ahead of you in line. Put your spouse's needs first, and others' missions before your own.

- Nehemiah sticks up for the poor who are being abused and taken advantage of (Neh. 5:1–13).
- Alan and Ann intentionally build relationships with others. They spend extra effort and energy loving their kids in tangible ways, especially when they react negatively to their parents' decisions about God's mission and what it will cost their family.

## Financial

Help to meet the basic needs of others before indulging in your own wants and desires. Be generous. When in doubt or when you see a need, give to someone else. (More on this in chapter 11.)

- Nehemiah chooses not to acquire more land (Neh. 5:16).
- Alan and Ann begin the sacrifice of not spending money on their own needs and comforts, redirecting that money toward God's mission.

## Health

Choose submission over satisfaction. Submit your body to God by maintaining a healthy lifestyle, using your hands, feet, heart, and mind to serve and honor Him.

- Nehemiah doesn't eat the rich food allotted to him as governor (Neh. 5:14).
- Alan and Ann give up the comfort foods to which they've grown accustomed.

## Professional

Choose service over opportunism. Be a servant-leader who is mindful of helping others get ahead in life.

- Nehemiah leaves the security of his high position as King Artexerxes's cupbearer to go repair Jerusalem (Neh. 2:1-10).
- Alan and Ann realize they're not equipped to handle some of the new things they will soon encounter professionally, so they sign up for extra classes to augment their knowledge.

## Home

Practice sharing instead of hoarding. Downsize your possessions. Share them with others.

- Nehemiah opens his home to hundreds of Jews, officials, and others from surrounding nations (Neh. 5:17-19).
- Alan and Ann decide to downsize their possessions and move to a place better suited to God's mission for their marriage.

## Big Dreams

Seek to surrender rather than control. Yield your heartfelt dreams and desires to God so He can align them with His best for you.

- Nehemiah completes his restoration project in only fifty-two days. (Jerusalem's walls had been in ruins for 150 years.)
- Through much sacrifice, Alan and Ann receive an opportunity to live out their dream of helping others read and understand God's Word.

Listening to Alan and Ann speak, we noticed something about their discovery process that we want to pass along to you as this chapter closes. When they started out, they had absolutely no clue as to what God's mission entailed.

"We just kept trying a bunch of new things," Alan stated. "With each one, God seemed to close a door as if to say, 'No, this isn't My mission for you.'"

Ann continued, "So we just kept going until we walked through the one door that stayed open. Because I'd committed to journaling about the experience, I could look back over my journal and see that God was using every shut door to lead us to the open one."

Understanding and applying God's Law of Inversion are pivotal to discovering His mission for your marriage. When your joint pursuit of God and His mission are exhibited by faithfully living out this OPORD in each of the seven marriage sectors, watch for opportunities to stretch your faith. That's the topic of the next chapter.

---

## Pray Together

Gracious God, we worship You. Your ways and thoughts are so much higher and greater than ours. Jesus, You came to invert the ways of the world. We desire to emulate You and the ways You went against the grain for Your glory and our good. We ask for Your wisdom to help us voluntarily invert every sector of our marriage. As we read and study the Bible, give us a deeper understanding of how You carried out Your life. Protect us from the enemy, who will tug against this process. Give us the courage, faith, and fortitude to submit to You. May our marriage and the lives of others be impacted for Your kingdom. In Jesus's name. Amen.

---

## Taking the Next Step

Use these questions as discussion points. You may also wish to record some answers or insights in your journal.

1. Can you think of another story in the Bible that demonstrates God's Law of Inversion? What was the long-term impact?
2. Share an experience when you went against the norm and chose to make a sacrifice rather than being selfish.

3. If you've finished a draft of your marriage mission statement, examine it for evidence of God's Law of Inversion. In other words, how might you exhibit inverse actions, behaviors, and attitudes through your mission?

## Chapter 10

# Your Marriage Mission Creed

*There will always be the unknown. There will always be
the unprovable. But faith confronts those frontiers with a
thrilling leap. Then life becomes vibrant with adventure!*
—ROBERT SCHULLER, *Tough Minded Faith for Tender Hearted People*

In a world run by blueprints, plans, and protocols, it can feel almost irresponsible not to have a plan B for every plan A. But, if you search the Bible, you won't find a shred of evidence that God asks His people for their backup plan. Instead He asks them to demonstrate faith. Living out an upside-down faith is never easy and often not clear cut, but God *is* very clear about how He expects us to respond.

To visually remind us of the importance of walking in faith during our overseas mission to the Holy Land, I (Penny) took a black permanent marker to a pair of tennis shoes. On the tip of my left shoe I wrote the word *plan*, and on the tip of my right shoe I wrote the word *faith*. *Plan faith* became our special code, denoting a desire to exercise faith with every step of our mission, especially when there was no clear-cut outline or plan.

Joshua and the Israelites were not given any sort of a detailed plan about their mission to enter and possess the Promised Land. Instead they were instructed to meditate on God's Word, which at that time would have been the first five books of the Old Testament: "Keep this Book of the Law always on your lips; meditate on it day and night, so that you may be careful to do everything written in it. Then you will be prosperous and successful. Have I not commanded you? Be strong and courageous. Do not be afraid; do not be discouraged, for the LORD your God will be with you wherever you go" (Josh. 1:8–9).

God's people were also instructed to faithfully obey all His commands (Josh. 1:7). Doing so guaranteed a successful mission. They were to act in faith based on what they believed. If that was true then, and if God's Word is timeless, then why would it be any different today? It's God's desire that, as with the Israelites long ago, your daily actions and interactions would be based on what you believe. Your acts of faith—your fulfillment of your mission—stem from your beliefs. So what do you believe?

What do you believe about your mission, your God, your marriage? Do you have a written list of those beliefs? If you don't, you're in danger of falling into the enemy's many traps. (More information on the enemy's traps will be covered in the Hazards and Hostiles phase.)

## CREATING A CREED OF BELIEF

Every military branch of the Unites States has a creed—an affirmation of values and convictions and a code of conduct. The statements contained in military creeds serve as standards to guide all plans, decisions, actions, and reactions. The creeds are often recited at the conclusion of training or during public ceremonies. They also serve as a succinct profession of faith in times of both peace and peril. Because each branch of the military is unique, the creed adopted for each one is different from the others.

Military groups aren't the only ones to live by creeds. Perhaps you are familiar with the Apostles' Creed, often recited in liturgical churches. The word *creed* is derived from the Latin word *credo*, which means, "I believe." While the Apostles' Creed has been translated and altered by various religious sects, it can best be described as a statement of beliefs for the Christian faith. Here is a common rendering.

## The Apostles' Creed

I believe in God, the Father almighty,
    creator of heaven and earth.

I believe in Jesus Christ, God's only Son, our Lord,
    who was conceived by the Holy Spirit,
    born of the Virgin Mary,
    suffered under Pontius Pilate,
    was crucified, died, and was buried;
    he descended to the dead.
    On the third day he rose again;
    he ascended into heaven,
    he is seated at the right hand of the Father,
    and he will come again to judge the living and the dead.

I believe in the Holy Spirit,
    the holy catholic and apostolic church,
    the communion of saints,
    the forgiveness of sins,
    the resurrection of the body,
    and the life everlasting. Amen.

## RULES OF ENGAGEMENT

Like the church of Jesus Christ and the branches of the armed forces, a marriage on God's mission also needs a creed. Its professions, in alignment with God's Word, serve as your rules of engagement, the OPORDs by which you function each day.

Because your marriage and your mission are unique, your creed needs to be something the two of you create together to express that uniqueness. A marriage mission creed is made up of a "we believe" statement for each of the seven sectors of marriage, and it includes a verse or passage of Scripture to anchor it in God's Word. Here is an example:

- Spiritual—We believe in putting God first in our lives by meeting alone with Him each morning and weekly as a couple (Prov. 2:1–11).
- Relational—We believe in actively nurturing love, grace, and forgiveness in our marriage and in all other relationships (Col. 3:12–15).
- Financial—We believe in faithfully giving a monthly tithe and extra offerings to God with generous hearts (Prov. 3:9–10).
- Health—We believe in treating our bodies as God's temples, keeping them fit, active, and healthy (1 Cor. 6:19–20).
- Professional—We believe in exercising all professional affairs with a servant model of humility (Matt. 20:25–28).
- Home—We believe in maintaining our home as a refuge for ourselves and a place of peace, blessing, and sanctuary for others (Isa. 32:17–18).
- Big dreams—We believe in dreaming with God and acting on our belief that all things are possible with Him (Mark 9:23).

Keep in mind that your mission flows from your marriage. Therefore, every sector of your marriage impacts your mission, and your mission will often impact every sector of your marriage.

In the same way that your one-sentence marriage mission statement takes time to hone and craft, it will take time to develop your marriage mission creed. Ask God to lead you to the verses or passages of the Bible on which to base every sector of your marriage, and discuss how you want each sector to represent what the Bible teaches.

Over time, your creed will become your "us"—who you are as a couple and what you stand for. It will serve as the grid through which you view all the circumstances of your life together, how you carry out God's mission, how you solve problems, and most importantly, how you approach matters that require faith. Remember, it's always faith (acting out your beliefs) that matters most to God. Always. Therefore, God will orchestrate circumstances to stretch and grow your faith in all seven sectors of your marriage.

## EXECUTING PLAN FAITH

So how do you exercise plan faith in each of the seven sectors of a marriage pursuing God's mission? It depends on your marriage and your creed. Using the sample marriage mission creed below, let's consider a scenario where faith might be both challenged and exercised in each of the seven sectors. Keep in mind that a faith challenge isn't just about huge leaps or miraculous feats. God also requires faith in the small, everyday circumstances of life.

- Spiritual—We believe in putting God first in our lives by meeting alone with Him each morning and weekly as a couple (Prov. 2:1–11).

  Faith challenge: You are meeting with your spouse each week when a sudden change in employment rearranges your entire schedule. You're thrown out of your normal routine as the demands of the new job consume you. Do you give up meeting together with your spouse, or do you persevere and put forth the extra energy to figure out a new time to meet, and keep moving forward on God's mission?

- Relational—We believe in actively nurturing love, grace, and forgiveness in our marriage and in all other relationships (Col. 3:12–15).

  Faith challenge: A woman you considered to be a friend has openly spoken out against your marriage mission of tutoring at-risk neighborhood children. She feels your services should be geared to children inside the church, not outside. Do you confront her? Do you avoid her? Do you allow bitterness to take root and just blow her off? Or do you try to work through your differences in a healthy way, nurturing forgiveness and extending grace?

- Financial—We believe in faithfully giving a monthly tithe and extra offerings to God with generous hearts (Prov. 3:9–10).

  Faith challenge: Finances are tight during the holidays. You could really use some extra cash to buy Christmas gifts for your kids. Do you skip out on giving your monthly tithe so you'll have the extra money you need?

- Health—We believe in treating our bodies as God's temples, keeping them fit, active, and healthy (1 Cor. 6:19–20).

  Faith challenge: You hate going to the doctor and avoid doing so at all costs. However, you've been drastically losing weight over the past few months, and your spouse is concerned. Do you dismiss your spouse's concerns and excuse the weight loss as just a benign anomaly? Or do you heed your spouse's counsel and make an appointment with your family physician?

- Professional—We believe in exercising all professional affairs with a servant model of humility (Matt. 20:25–28).

   Faith challenge: You receive an award at work and need to write an acceptance speech. Do you direct attention to yourself and your own accomplishments, or do you humbly express gratitude to those who helped you achieve your success?

- Home—We believe in maintaining our home as a refuge for ourselves and a place of peace, blessing, and sanctuary for others (Isa. 32:17–18).

   Faith challenge: You are a domestically challenged wife who loathes entertaining others. Your husband feels led to invite colleagues over for dinner who do not have a personal relationship with God. Do you find a way to press beyond your own dislikes to be his helpmate and open your home for this gathering?

- Big dreams—We believe in dreaming with God and acting on our belief that all things are possible with Him (Mark 9:23).

   Faith challenge: Despite every attempt to get your writing published, you consistently receive rejection notices. Do you give up your dream of being a writer? Or do you find a way to improve your skills and keep refining and resubmitting your work?

Demonstrating greater faith through obedience to God and consistent meditation on His Word is the answer to every question in the examples you just read. In fact, greater faith is the answer to every question you'll face on God's mission. Problems—big and small—present you with opportunities to exercise faith, pray more fervently, and think more creatively. At times you may wonder whether you're being foolish or full of faith. It's no small feat to endure the insecurity of your surroundings and step out onto a path you cannot see. But when Christ returns, guess what He'll be looking for above all else? "When the Son of Man comes, will he find *faith* on the earth?" (Luke 18:8, italics added).

Our faith as Christians is not intended to be static but dynamic. Faith that is active is faith that is organic, ever growing, ever stretching, and ever increasing. Just when you think you've got the faith thing down pat, God will present you with an opportunity to believe Him to a greater degree. This is especially true about generosity, the topic of the next chapter. "When someone has been given much, much will be required in return; and when someone has been entrusted with much, even more will be required" (Luke 12:48 NLT).

Plan Faith, David and Cindy • *4:54 minutes*

Plan Faith, Pedro and Tania • *6:09 minutes*

---

## Pray Together

Heavenly Father, help us design our marriage mission creed. Lead us to the verses that will serve as the code of conduct for all seven sectors of our marriage. Give us the time and patience to develop a creed that will guide us as we walk out what we believe.

We need more faith, but we're not sure what it will take for our faith to grow. We also admit shying away from difficulties that often seem to be Your chosen method of stretching and growing our faith. Help our fear and unbelief! Teach us to place all our faith in You and not the people or plans of this world. Such things cannot sustain us, yet we tend to lean on what we can see rather than what we cannot. Grant us a greater measure of faith in all seven sectors of our marriage as we come together in prayer, read Your Word, and live out each day. In Jesus's name. Amen.

---

## Taking the Next Step

Use these questions as discussion points. You may also wish to record some answers or insights in your journal.

1. Begin a draft of your marriage mission creed. Select a verse or passage of Scripture for each of the seven sectors of marriage. Then write a one-sentence "we will" statement of belief. Take your time. You are not expected to complete this process in one sitting. Below are some sample "we will" statements to help you.

   - We will regularly attend church as a family.
   - We will give of our time and resources, including our finances.
   - We will love our enemies as well as those who love us.
   - We will make regular medical/dental/vision appointments and work to keep our bodies fit.
   - We will open our home to others.
   - We will do our best at our jobs, as working for God.
   - We will pray together every morning.
   - We will not give up on God's dreams for us.
   - We will spend quality time together as a family each week.

- We will closely monitor the shows our kids watch on TV and the sites they access on the Internet.

2. What has been the greatest step of faith you've ever taken in your life? In your marriage? Why were these things so monumental?

# Chapter 11

# Sharing Your Rations

*I have found that among its other benefits,*
*giving liberates the soul of the giver.*
—MAYA ANGELOU, "The Sweetness of Charity"

In the army, I was paid a salary of $200 a month. Each soldier was also given a ration card, which allowed us to buy things at the PX (post exchange) on base. Since the food I needed was supplied by either K-rations (daily combat food rations introduced by the army in WWII) or C-rations (individual canned or precooked food, mostly issued when fresh food, mess hall meals, or field kitchen food was not available), my basic expenses were covered. Therefore, I sent most of my salary home so my dad could deposit it in my savings account.

Given my experiences with rations in the military and my first real earnings, I learned some important economic principles such as living within my means, saving for the future, and being grateful I wasn't starving like many of the people in Vietnam. But the most humbling lessons came from the hungry children.

On many days, the Vietnamese children scampered alongside our vehicles shouting, "Peace! Peace!" their fingers making the V sign (the index and middle fingers extended and parted). Although the V sign was originally a sign of victory in the early 1940s, during the 1960s, and specifically the Vietnam War, this hand gesture was widely adopted as the counterculture symbol of peace. Although the children shouted "Peace!" and waved their hands, their distended stomachs screamed, "Food!"

The kids scrambled to grab the rations that the other GIs and I would toss from the side of our vehicles. With their tiny hands wrapped around each can or package, they smiled as though they had just been handed pure gold.

The Vietnamese children taught me two things: be grateful for what you get, and give from what you're given. Not until many years later would I realize that gratitude and generosity were also taught in the Bible: "Honor the LORD with your wealth, with the firstfruits of all your crops; then your barns will be filled to overflowing, and your vats will brim over with new wine" (Prov. 3:9–10).

## TYPES OF RATIONS

Each year, the Israelites were expected to give the priests the first part of all their crops (a tenth, to be exact), which consisted mostly of grain, wine, and oil. To those who brought God these tithes and offerings, He promised more in return.

Tithing is part of God's OPORD for giving and receiving. For several years Penny and I thought tithing only pertained to money. Over time and study, however, we discovered that God wanted us to give from our supply, not just our surplus. And there were four types of "rations" from which we could give: time, treasure, talent, and testimony. Here are some tangible examples of how tithing in these four areas might play out for you. The lists are by no means exhaustive, but they might jump-start your thinking.

### Tithing Your Time
  • Spend time with God first each day.
  • Memorize Scripture.

- Meet with a prayer partner.
- Pray for others.
- Journal.
- Study the Bible.
- Read Christian literature.
- Fast.
- Visit the sick.
- Volunteer your time.

## Tithing Your Treasure
- Tithe 10 percent of your income.
- Give over and above to special needs and causes.
- Adopt a family or person in need at Christmas.
- Adopt an orphan through a local or world missions program.

## Tithing Your Talent
- Repair something for widows, orphans, or an underprivileged group.
- Serve in a ministry at church.
- Offer your talents to someone in need of them.
- Make gifts for others.

## Tithing Your Testimony
- Share your testimony of salvation with someone.
- Tell stories about the things God has done in your life.
- Write encouraging notes to others telling of God's goodness.
- Share your struggles and victories humbly with others.
- Use your workplace as an opportunity to witness for Christ.

## OUTSIDE THE BOX

In basic training, like every other soldier, I had at the end of my bunk a footlocker that contained all my personal items. Inside the box, every item had its proper place. Socks were rolled up and put in one corner; my belt buckles were placed in another corner. We were not to keep any of our personal items outside the box, and each of our footlockers was to be locked whenever it wasn't in use. If any of us were caught with our boxes unlocked, the contents were dumped all over the floor, and we were severely humiliated and disciplined.

For many years after I was discharged, I applied that same foot-locker concept to my knowledge of God and His ways with regard to rations and possessions. Everything had its proper place. What was mine, was mine. I only had so much, so I kept it locked up tightly. Of course God had His section. But no one, including God, was allowed free rein with my personal items or space. I couldn't think or act outside that box with regard to material things, and I had no idea that God's OPORDs for giving should not be constrained or contained.

My lockbox mentality changed when Penny and I began living out God's mission for our marriage. Together we learned the importance of thinking, praying, and giving outside the box—that is, without limiting God to our finite understanding and personal limitations.

For example, in the days and nights before we left on our first forty-day marriage mission trip across the United States, God began outgiving us. People from church dropped by with care packages and donations—enough to cover the first part of our cross-country trip. Others contacted people along our route to set up housing. Another ministry we'd become acquainted with donated a wireless card for our laptop. One couple who had been spiritually fueling our mission since its inception stopped by to anoint us with oil and pray with us. By the end of the trip, all our expenses were covered, and we even had a little money left over.

Thinking, praying, and giving outside the box also means anticipating and expecting miracles. The Bible contains several passages that exemplify this idea:

> "What no eye has seen, what no ear has heard, and what no human mind has conceived"—the things God has prepared for those who love him. (1 Cor. 2:9)

> Now to him who is able to do immeasurably more than all we ask or imagine, according to his power that is at work within us . . . (Eph. 3:20)

> "For my thoughts are not your thoughts, neither are your ways my ways," declares the LORD. "As the heavens are higher than the earth, so are my ways higher than your ways and my thoughts than your thoughts." (Isa. 55:8–9)

God's creativity and ability are endless in every area of a marriage on God's mission. His OPORDs are, at times, completely unfathomable. In a very literal sense, God's ways are beyond description! For His people to follow His outside-the-box OPORDs, God often orchestrates a circumstance of desperate need. In other words, He teaches us about His infinite abilities by asking us to conquer impossible things and give more than we have set aside to give. The enlargement of our emptiness and the exaggeration of our ache create all the more room for God, not humans, to fill those needs. Our impossible needs make room for the God of the impossible.

## GOD OF THE IMPOSSIBLE

Every great mission from God is cultivated and carried out within a habitat of impossibility. Impossibility is where miracles bud and burst forth. Let's look at several examples of couples in the Bible who faced the unthinkable and received a miracle.

### Abraham and Sarah (Gen. 17)

- *Mission*: To be exceedingly fruitful (v. 2) so that nations would come from their union and God's covenant would be established for all generations (vv. 7–9).
- *Impossibility*: How could a barren old woman get pregnant? But steeped in sheer faith, Abraham and Sarah believed they would be fruitful even in their old age, even in a strange new land, and even with no idea of their destination.

### Joseph and Mary (Matt. 1:18–25)

- *Mission*: To give birth to and parent the Savior of the world.
- *Impossibility*: How do you parent God's Son? When Jesus was born, Herod wanted to kill Him. Yet Joseph and Mary moved as God led and raised Jesus in their own home.

### Priscilla and Aquila (Acts 18)

- *Mission*: Spread the gospel and help establish the early church.
- *Impossibility*: How would Priscilla and Aquila carry out God's will to spread the gospel alongside the apostle Paul? They were believing Jews ordered to leave Italy by Emperor Claudius. By trade Priscilla and Aquila were tentmakers, not evangelists. Yet they became major players in making disciples.

Each of these biblical duos faced at least one impossible circumstance. Their difficulties brought them to the end of themselves, their abilities, and their provisions, forcing them to exercise the one thing that would make all the difference: faith.

Are you straining hard to look beyond your own impossible circumstance and what seems like God's baffling lack of activity? One of your most important strategies in the present is to look back at miracles from the past and appeal to the God who performed them: "Then I thought, 'To this I will appeal: the years when the Most High stretched out his right hand. I will remember the deeds of the LORD; yes, I will remember your miracles of long ago. I will consider all your works and meditate on all your mighty deeds'" (Ps. 77:10–12).

Meditating on God's past miracles takes your eyes off what you do not have and what God is not doing. It also increases your faith. Some of the miracles recorded in Scripture—the ones that have had the greatest impact on us—remind us that our God is the God of the impossible:

- The once-barren womb (1 Sam. 1:1–20)
- The ram in the thicket (Gen. 22:1–19)
- The well-fed wanderers (Exod. 16)
- Gideon's fleece (Judg. 6:36–40)
- The widow's oil (2 Kings 4:1–7)
- Breath-filled bones (Ezek. 37:1–14)
- The floating ax head (2 Kings 6:1–7)
- The prophet's fire (1 Kings 18:16–46)
- The fiery furnace (Dan. 3)
- The virgin birth (Matt. 1:18–25)
- Water becoming wine (John 2:1–12)
- The healed paralytic (Matt. 9:1–8)
- The stilled tempest (Matt. 8:23–27)
- The risen brother (John 11:1–44)
- The demoniacs' deliverance (Matt. 8:28–34)
- Death's power destroyed (Matt. 28:1–10; Rev. 21:1–4)

If God did these things back then, He can do them right now too! He can cure cancer, return wayward children, supply money, create contacts. He can do *all* things. In the list of miracles you just read, each impossibility involved different people at different times in different circumstances. But all the miracles had one thing in common: faith.

Still think God can't or won't work for you in your present-day problem? Right here, right now? If God is so fully able to do the impossible, why do we dread impossibilities? Because, let's be honest, we do. What a blessing, then, to know that God works with what faith we have despite our trembling hearts. Let us illustrate with an example from our own marriage.

I (Clint) had amassed some debt before Penny and I got remarried. Due to my financial mismanagement during the years I had wandered from God, I also had an IRS debt that had to be cleared up. It was ugly. We made an appointment with a Christian accountant we could trust. On the day of the appointment, we pulled into the parking lot of his office a few minutes early so we could pray together.

"I'm dreading this appointment," I confessed to Penny. "There will be huge financial penalties for being delinquent. This whole thing is an impossible mess." I took her hand in mine and began to pray.

"God, I've already admitted to You and Penny that I destroyed my financial life over the last several years. Please help us clean up this mess together. You are the God of the impossible, but my faith is small. Give us the grace to deal with the consequences of my actions by paying whatever penalties are due. We ask for a miracle. In Jesus's name. Amen."

I (Penny) was sincerely moved as Clint prayed so vulnerably in the cab of the truck. I knew his greatest fear was that in attempting to clear up his financial issues, we'd sink even deeper into a hole of debt with no visible way out.

While our accountant shuffled papers, asked questions, and crunched numbers, Clint's face turned ashy gray. The anxiety was overwhelming. Our impossible circumstances revealed our helpless human state and forced us to fully depend on God. After several hours, our accountant slowly slid a single piece of folded paper across his desk and leaned back in his chair.

"Okay," he said, "taking everything into account, here's your bottom line."

With much hesitation, we leaned forward and unfolded the paper. Like two ice cubes, we were completely frozen by the final total.

Our accountant broke the silence.

"Well, what do you think?"

We *couldn't* think. We were in shock. We did not owe the IRS money. The IRS owed us, over fifteen thousand dollars! Our accountant went on to explain. "There were many errors in Clint's paperwork from the last several years, and there were credits that were unaccounted for." We hardly heard a word he said.

When we got back in the truck, we cried and thanked God, completely astounded by what He had done with our impossible situation. And that's not all. As we continued asking Him to take our finances outside the box and to do impossible things, we found ourselves debt-free within one year, except for our mortgage payment. Then a few years later, God eliminated that as well.

Once God performed those financial miracles, we began to more fervently seek Him about the other six sectors of a marriage on His mission. Getting sucked into status-quo faith was no longer an option.

Is there a sector of your marriage mission that God wants to take outside the box to increase your faith and His glory? Are you faced with an impossible situation? Have you stuck God in a footlocker and thrown away the key? Have you packaged any aspect of Him in your own finite places, spaces, and prayers?

One of the most powerful ways to bust every lockbox wide open is to make a list of your impossibilities and pray over them when you meet to read this book each week. Doing so will lead you on a course to prove that not only can God break the lid off your footlocker but faith will be the means to access all you need and more.

Facing impossibilities together is a normal and necessary part of the process as you set out to pursue God and discover His mission. You must let God use all your concerns, questions, and impossibilities as a catalyst for deeper faith. Like gas in a car, the impossibility of your circumstances fuels your faith. God will change either your circumstance or your heart toward it, or sometimes both.

Do you know the God of the impossible? Maybe you haven't been placed in an impossible situation yet. You will, and it will be one of the hardest times in your marriage. Relief relentlessly beckons you to scramble and find another way to meet the need on your own. If you don't regularly acquaint and reacquaint yourself with the God of the impossible, you'll raise a white flag and surrender or settle for something less than His best.

Throughout the Bible there is evidence that God not only likes impossibilities but actually orchestrates them, then basks in their fulfillment and in your increased faith. For you to recognize your need for God, His mission must be much bigger than what the two of you could ever accomplish on your own. Impossibility is simply the proper prerequisite for God to do great things.

 God of the Impossible, Eugene and Ruth • *3:47 minutes*

## Pray Together

Father, we acknowledge that You want us to give from *all* our rations, not just our finances. Show us the meaning of giving our time, treasure, talent, and testimony back to You in worship. Reveal the places where we're selfish, and grant us generous hearts that give selflessly. Examine all seven sectors of our marriage, and show us tangible ways to give, think, and pray without limiting You. As we give from each area, please multiply and bless these rations. Stretch our resources to accomplish Your will. As we read about Your miracles in the past, fill us with the faith to expect miracles in the present. In any areas where we're reluctant to give, stir our hearts to be generous with no strings attached. You know what we need, not what we think we need. Your power is limitless; Your ability, endless; Your worth, matchless; Your Word, timeless. We declare all these things to be true. In Jesus's name. Amen.

---

## Taking the Next Step

Use these questions as discussion points. You may also wish to record some answers or insights in your journal.

1. Discuss tangible ways you can tithe from the following rations: time, treasure, talent, and testimony.
2. Does giving from your rations trigger any fears and worries? Name or describe them specifically.
3. Make a list of your impossible circumstances—things that seem to be standing in the way of your marriage and/or God's mission. Compare the list with your spouse's list. Look for similarities and differences. Join your lists together into one list and pray over it each week. (Note: You may differ from your spouse as to what you consider an impossibility. Validate each other's thoughts, even if you don't share them.)
4. As you look back at the biblical duos listed on page 126, what similarities, generalizations, or truths can you apply to your marriage? Which duo do you most identify with, and why?
5. As you look back at the list of miracles on page 127, which one speaks to your own faith most loudly, and why?

Chapter 12

# Active Duty

*Each of us may be sure that if God sends us on stony*
*paths He will provide us with strong shoes.*
—ALEXANDER MACLAREN, "Shod for the Road"

You've spent the last several chapters examining God's OPORDs in connection with His mission for your marriage. The main principles in those prior chapters—God's Law of Inversion, plan faith, and sharing your rations—have generally highlighted God's open-ended nature—His creativity and limitlessness—rather than His more linear and succinct traits. Our goal has been to convey the fact that God's OPORDs are beyond both your natural comprehension and your ability.

Having said that, God is also a God of order and detail. He is not chaotic or random. His protocols are divinely planned and perfectly executed. God also knows His children can only handle so much creativity. We need structure and strategy too. We need to know exactly what action to take next. We need a plan of action. The Bible says, "What good is it, my brothers and sisters, if someone claims to have faith but has no deeds? Can such faith save them? Suppose a brother or a sister is without clothes and daily food. If one of you says to them, 'Go in peace; keep warm and well fed,' but does nothing about their physical needs, what good is it? In the same way, faith by itself, if it is not accompanied by action, is dead" (James 2:14–17).

## WHAT'S THE PLAN OF ACTION?

Every successful mission carried out during my service in Vietnam was made up of a series of precise steps. These missions were vital and had to be carried out with exact order. The same is true for your marriage mission. The Bible teaches that the plans of the heart belong to you, but the answer comes from God (Prov. 16:1). Let us help you make some plans in three important areas related to your mission: people, permissions, and provisions. We'll look again to Nehemiah and his mission to repair the walls of Jerusalem for our examples. Nehemiah needed a strategy for dealing with all three areas to successfully carry out his assigned task.

### People

Nehemiah's mission mainly involved the Jews in Jerusalem. However, because he left his job as cupbearer to King Artaxerxes (Neh. 2), the king, his queen, and others in the kingdom of Persia were also involved and impacted.

### Permissions

While the Bible does not give details about all the permissions Nehemiah may have needed to execute such a monumental building project, it does say that he first sought permission from God through prayer (Neh. 1:4–11). Then, he asked permission from King Artaxerxes to take a leave of absence from his regular job (Neh. 2:5). He also needed letters from various public officials (Neh. 2:7–9).

### Provisions

Nehemiah needed time, food, water, tools, timber, stone, and many other types of building materials to repair the city's walls and gates.

He and the workers also needed spears, shields, bows, and armor to protect themselves from their enemies (Neh. 4:16).

Now that you've considered the people, permissions, and provisions needed by Nehemiah, take some time to answer the questions below. To spur your thinking, begin by copying your marriage mission statement here. Update it if necessary.

_____

_____

Now let's look more deeply at each of the three areas, one by one. Record your progress in your journal.

## People
*While every mission requires action in various ways, it also requires people. In the prompts below, be as specific as possible in identifying people who will be involved in or impacted by your mission.*

- List the main people group(s) your mission will serve (neighborhood children, the homeless, pastors, widows, businesswomen, etc.).
- List any secondary group(s) your mission may also end up serving (people who may benefit even though they are not your main target).
- Whom will you need to help you carry out your mission (financial supporters, co-laborers, leaders, etc.)?
- Which people or groups might be resistant to your mission (neighbors, family, coworkers, churches, city officials, etc.)?
- Which people might serve as a cheering squad to encourage your mission?
- Who might be willing to donate their time, treasure, talent, or testimony to your mission?

- How will you get the word out to other people about your mission (networking, building relationships, social media, news media, etc.)?

## Permissions
*Every mission requires certain permissions. Be as specific as possible in planning out the permissions your mission will require.*

- First and foremost, you need God's permission to carry out your marriage mission. In what way(s) do you expect or hope God will confirm His permission for you to move forward?
- What legal permissions does your mission require (government regulations, policies, insurance, facility-use permits, building space, building permits, storage space, etc.)?
- What informal permissions do you need to obtain (pastor, church, or other interest groups)?

## Provisions
*Every mission needs specific supplies, funding, equipment, tools, materials, and space.*

- List any supplies your mission will require (office supplies, food, clothing, tools, equipment, etc.).
- What training might be needed to carry out your mission (degrees, workshops, classes, etc.)?
- Make a list of items you would like to have donated toward your mission. Remember to think outside the box.

## ACTION STEPS
Based on what you listed for the people, permissions, and provisions needed, you can now prioritize some short-term action steps. For each of the three areas, write one measurable goal. Limit your

goals to ones you can easily accomplish over the next thirty to forty-five days. We've provided an example for each area based on the following marriage mission: *We will serve widows and single mothers by mowing their lawns and doing basic yard work.* Below each example, write your own goal with *your* marriage mission statement in mind.

## People

Example goal: Contact John and Jane Smith to see if they can help secure teens to serve on a rotating yard work crew.

Your goal:

## Permissions

Example goal: Research any liability issues for working on other people's property with their permission.

Your goal:

## Provisions

Example goal: Clean out our garage and inventory the condition of the lawn mower, edger, blower, and other gardening tools.

Your goal:

If you've completed all the exercises in the chapter so far, well done! You've taken some important steps forward. Your next big step is simply to accomplish the three goals you've identified over the next thirty to forty-five days. To avoid procrastinating or taking on too much too soon at this stage of your mission, here are a few tips.

## AVOID MARCHING IN PLACE

New missions often have a euphoric beginning, but then, for various reasons, they quickly fizzle. You find yourself marching in place, moving but not getting anywhere. Avoiding the following common potholes will help you continue a forward march.

*Start small, pray big.* Your prayers must be bigger than your plans. Setting up a bunch of lofty goals can set you up for failure right from the get-go. Instead, saturate every step of your mission in prayer. Ask others to pray for you. Rely more on prayer than on your plans.

*Honor military secrets.* There's a reason that inside information is supposed to stay inside. With the explosion of social media, you may find it tempting to broadcast to the world what you plan to do and exactly how you plan to do it. However, this can present added difficulties early on, such as negative opinions or reactions from others. Think carefully about which details you share with whom, especially in the beginning stages. As a general rule, be conservative in your communication of the details for now.

*Stick to your mission.* It's easy to let your mission run wild and become something other than what God has assigned to you. Look at everything you're doing through the lens of your marriage mission statement.

*Keep your expectations on God.* Rely on God first and foremost. Even well-meaning people can disappoint you. Extend grace to those who don't meet your expectations or make promises but fail to fulfill them.

*Know your rank.* Your marriage mission is in its infancy. Like GIs who have just arrived in a foreign land, you're newbies, not veterans. Know your position and use it to learn from others who have been out in the field longer than you.

*Hold plans loosely.* Your plans need to be flexible. Things change. Resiliency develops when you are willing to change too. Sometimes

God will even frustrate your plans (Ps. 33:10) to force a delay or change.

*Remember your creed.* Your marriage mission creed contains the statement of beliefs by which you live and serve. Become increasingly familiar with it. Memorize it. Post it or frame it in a prominent place.

Your marriage mission may not be as dialed in as you'd like it to be right now. If you couldn't fill in all the planning spaces in this chapter, that's okay. What counts is that you do the best you can with what you have.

 Do What You Can, Rob and Panda • *3:55 minutes*

Quoting a proverb he learned in the military, the late president Dwight D. Eisenhower once said, "Plans are worthless, but planning is everything."[3] Those are words to ponder. There are things you can plan for and things you cannot. God's mission will include unpredictable opposing enemy forces (if it hasn't already). Remember, you are equipped. You are not taking a pocketknife to a gunfight; you carry a loaded weapon, and you have a full arsenal of heavy artillery at your disposal.

---

## Pray Together

God, our desire is to keep marching forward on Your mission. Help us set goals that are in alignment with Your will for us. Keep us focused. We give You permission to change or rearrange our plans and goals. Our mission needs people, permissions, and provisions. We place all our expectations for those things on You. Release Your favor to go before us and pave the way for what needs to get done. May everything we do bring You honor. In Jesus's name. Amen.

## Taking the Next Step

Use these questions as discussion points. You may also wish to record some answers or insights in your journal.

1. This chapter helped you set measurable goals in three different areas: people, permissions, and provisions. Which of those three areas is the most difficult for you to deal with as an individual? As a couple? Why do you think this is?
2. Mark your calendar for forty-five days from today as the due date to accomplish the three goals you wrote down in this chapter. Discuss who will be responsible for each goal (or you may decide to work on all three goals together).
3. Review your marriage mission creed and make any necessary revisions. Create a simple poster or an enlarged, framed reproduction of your creed, and hang it in a prominent place. Keep in mind that as your mission progresses, you may still find the need for future revisions.

*Phase IV*

# HAZARDS AND HOSTILES

## Chapter 13

# Know Your Enemy

*Conquering any difficulty always gives one*
*a secret joy, for it means pushing back a*
*boundary-line and adding to one's liberty.*
—HENRI FREDERIC AMIEL, *Private Journal*

You may wince at the title of this chapter, because no one really wants to know their enemies. Knowing indicates familiarity, and frankly, who wants to be familiar with someone dead-set against you? However, if you don't know how Satan works or believe that he will stop at nothing to abort your mission, you won't stand a fighting chance against him.

The ancient Chinese military strategist Sun Tzu once wrote, "If you know the enemy and know yourself, you need not fear the result of a hundred battles. If you know yourself but not the enemy, for every victory gained you will also suffer a defeat. If you know neither the enemy nor yourself, you will succumb in every battle."[4]

In the army, it was the job of my commanding officers to do their homework on our enemy. Military strategies were planned and executed based on our officers' knowledge of how the North Vietnamese fought and functioned. Even though I was not a high-ranking officer, after spending two tours serving in Nam, I knew more than I ever wanted to know about the Viet Cong, or "Charlie," as we called them.

The goal of this chapter is to help you get to know your enemy and his main offensive tactic: marital division. Satan's strategy is to divide and conquer. God's strategy is to unite and fight. Satan wants to split you into enemy camps, one against the other, and he will relentlessly attempt to do so. But God promises to give you the firepower you need through faith in Jesus Christ. In this chapter we'll look at two main ways Satan will try to cause division in a marriage on God's mission.

Two types of barriers can cause division in your marriage: external barriers, which block your marriage from without, and internal barriers, which block it from within. Both kinds are erected by Satan to get spouses to fight each other instead of uniting against him. Remember your people, permissions, and provisions planning from the previous chapter? Your barrier or roadblock might be a person who speaks out against your mission, a permission you need but cannot obtain, or a provisional gap, as in finances.

To illustrate the difference between internal and external barriers, we will use two examples from Joshua's mission to lead the Israelites into the Promised Land.

## EXTERNAL BARRIERS: CROSSING THE JORDAN RIVER

The Jordan River was a roadblock that could have stopped the nation of Israel in its tracks. To get to the Promised Land, it had to be crossed. Then once it was, God's people would face their enemies head-on. No escape. No turning back.

The Jordan wasn't just a small, trickling tributary; it was a roaring body of water at flood stage (Josh. 3:15). Think about the moment when God's people stood at its overflowing banks—at least forty thousand fighting men from two and a half of the twelve Israelite tribes (Josh. 4:13). That number doesn't include the fighting men in the tribes not mentioned as well as women, children, and men unfit for battle. It's safe to assume that some of the people were thrilled by the adventure and conquest of crossing the river, while others wanted to turn tail and run. Division.

The difficult and dangerous task of crossing the Jordan River symbolizes external barriers that must be crossed to fulfill your marriage mission. Perhaps your mission to set up food stations for the homeless requires a permit from the city, and your application for that permit gets declined. You've hit an external barrier. External barriers are those problems that exist outside of yourselves and pack the power to cause division between you.

Sometimes external barriers ignite discord because you're at one end of the spectrum about how to cross the barrier and your spouse is at the other. Both of you think you're right, but something's got to give, and neither of you wants to budge an inch. For instance, Clint and I were in the midst of our own plans when we received news that a dear friend's family crisis had drastically escalated. I wanted to immediately run to the rescue. Clint, on the other hand, insisted that we wait and pray.

"This is no time to wait!" I insisted. "This is part of our mission and our friend is hurting. We need to go and help now." Clint held his ground. Our differences ignited all measure of emotion, and each word put more distance between us. Our external barrier quickly became an impasse.

How do you make ends meet when a situation like this occurs in your marriage? How do you not allow an external barrier to road-block you from moving forward together?

We followed the priests' example at the Jordan River. They entered the floodwaters with no visible path through it. The waters had not rolled back first, as they had done at the crossing of the Red Sea. Instead, the priests stepped into the Jordan's unparted waters—but they were not alone. The ark—symbolizing the holy presence of God

Almighty—went before the Israelites and remained there in the Jordan's channel until everyone had crossed over.

Clint and I didn't have an ark. But we did have the cross of Christ and the Holy Spirit, as do you. The two of us sat together in those murky waters of disagreement and impasse, but we were not alone. God was between us. Clint explained why he felt the way he did, and I listened. I explained the way I felt, and Clint listened. Although we still couldn't understand each other's opinions, we prayed together, asking God not to remove the barrier so much as to change our hearts toward it and toward each other. And He did. Honest discussion and united prayer helped us move toward a middle ground instead of splitting apart.

*Every* external barrier that threatens to divide you has already been crossed and crushed by the presence of the resurrected Christ. Every single one. As significant as the crossing of the Jordan was back then is the truth it symbolizes for you today: you must be willing to step into the floodwaters. But Christ goes into that danger ahead of you. His death and resurrection allow you to cross over the external barrier and into new territory together.

When you find yourselves facing a barrier or standing with your arms folded at opposite ends of a situation, bring those things to the cross in confession, surrender, and prayer. Keeping your differences in the dark allows bitterness, anger, and animosity to fester and grow like deadly black mold. Instead of pushing each other away, draw closer together. Honestly acknowledge your differences, and ask the Holy Spirit to reconcile them and even fuse them together.

Reconciling Your Differences, Dennis and Denise •
*2:23 minutes*

Be open to correction, change, and forgiveness, both seeking it and extending it. Instead of trying to change your spouse, be willing to let God change your own mind and heart. Expect to hear from God, and allow the power of the cross to generate unity and intimacy from the very same barriers the enemy wants to use to exaggerate your differences. Then, while your differences may collide, they won't explode and do harm. Instead, they'll meld together through the power of the cross and pave the way ahead for good. And in the process, you'll learn more about how your spouse ticks.

Crossing a marriage Jordan is also symbolic of leaving something old behind and entering something new together. When you think about it, the Israelites didn't cross the Jordan and enter into the Promised Land by anything *they* did. Yes, they took a step of faith, but they crossed the Jordan because the presence of God went before them into the danger and tarried there until it passed. This is how you'll be able to cross every marriage Jordan. The power and peace of God's presence will hold back the floodwaters from overwhelming you.

Having said all that, sometimes, oddly enough, it is God who erects a barrier or roadblock. His purpose might be to protect you, get you to change course, or increase your faith. These are all good things, though they may not feel that great at the time, and God's reasoning may be hard to understand. That's where trust must kick in. Proverbs 3:5–6 is a promise to cling to: "Trust in the LORD with all your heart and lean not on your own understanding; in all your ways submit to him, and he will make your paths straight."

It takes time, prayer, wisdom, and experience in discernment to decipher whether a barrier is erected by God or Satan. When a barrier is erected by God, Satan will always try to discourage and divide you through the magnitude of what you're facing. Remember the chapter about impossibilities? God orchestrates them, and Satan will try to ambush and defeat you through them. A general rule to

remember is, God always erects barriers for good, and Satan does so
for evil.

## INTERNAL BARRIERS: THE WALLS OF JERICHO

The barriers facing the Israelites didn't disappear once they crossed
the Jordan. They would also march smack dab into Jericho's fortified
walls. Jericho was an enemy stronghold that had to be completely
destroyed. It was a pagan settlement and the center of worship for
their moon god. Archaeologists speculate the name *Jericho* means
"moon city." Its inhabitants were engaged in idolatry, an ongoing
pattern of internal sinful behavior. Thus, Jericho symbolizes an
*internal* barrier—something inside your marriage such as an addiction or a pattern of unhealthy thinking that must be removed.

If Joshua and the Israelites could not conquer Jericho, Joshua
couldn't carry out God's mission. In addition, God's people would
not be able to move in and take full ownership of the land He had
given them. In the same way, strongholds can hinder you from living out your mission the way God intends. Strongholds keep you
bound to the enemy instead of living in the freedom Christ offers.
In the life of believers today, common internal strongholds include
things like idolatry, power, egotism, greed, self-gratification, addiction, unforgiveness, judgment, legalism, generational sin, and unbelief. In one way or another, each of these internal Jerichos can create
division.

For example, Tom and his wife pastored a small rural church. On
the outside, they were living out God's mission; inside their home,
Tom battled fits of uncontrollable rage. His explosive anger drove
his wife into periods of retreat. She wanted him to get help, but Tom
disagreed. He knew that if they exposed his problem, their position
in the church would be negatively impacted. Tom's internal Jericho
erected marital division. Eventually, his wife walked out.

Like the fortified city of Jericho, strongholds such as addiction or other skewed patterns of thinking or relating are internal barriers that must be totally destroyed. But how? A look back at God's unconventional battle plan to conquer Jericho will help answer that question.

> Now the gates of Jericho were securely barred because of the Israelites. No one went out and no one came in.
>
> Then the LORD said to Joshua, "See, I have delivered Jericho into your hands, along with its king and its fighting men. March around the city once with all the armed men. Do this for six days. Have seven priests carry trumpets of rams' horns in front of the ark. On the seventh day, march around the city seven times, with the priests blowing the trumpets. When you hear them sound a long blast on the trumpets, have the whole army give a loud shout; then the wall of the city will collapse and the army will go up, everyone straight in." (Josh. 6:1–5)

Can you imagine how God's plan for conquest must have sounded to the Israelites? How do you think Joshua's army received the news that instead of fighting their enemies with weapons, they were going to fight with faith? Do you think they were all in wholehearted agreement with God's plan? More than likely there was division as to what they should do and how they should do it. Regardless of what they might have thought, the people united in faith and obedience and forged ahead. The results were earthshaking: "When the trumpets sounded, the army shouted, and at the sound of the trumpet, when the men gave a loud shout, the wall collapsed; so everyone charged straight in, and they took the city" (Josh. 6:20).

Despite God's odd instructions, the Jews believed and obeyed. Like hand-to-hand combat, faith and obedience are a one-two punch in the face of every Jericho you'll encounter and the means by which you will take full possession of new territory on your mission—terrain that once belonged to your enemies.

But how exactly do you and your spouse unite and fight together instead of pulling apart? By drawing on the weapons of your faith. Think of the seven sectors of marriage we've discussed in this book: spiritual, relational, financial, health, professional, home, and big dreams. Next, name an internal barrier or stronghold—an area of skewed thinking or relating inside yourself (stick to yourself and not your spouse) that arises in one of those sectors. Now, drawing on your weapons of God's Word and prayer, follow these steps of faith and obedience:

- Name the internal barrier or stronghold.
- Identify its source.
- Locate a Scripture verse/passage to pray over your problem.
- Pray together about the steps of obedience and faith God is directing you to take.
- Thank God for using the barrier to unite you.

Following are examples of how you might apply this process to barriers in three different sectors.

## Spiritual

*Internal barrier*: Pride. I feel that I have to demonstrate a high degree of spiritual achievement to gain God's approval and the accolades of others.

*Source*: My relationship with my parents and their high expectations for me as a child skewed my thinking and self-worth. Because of this, I tend to look for approval from others or from what I do for people.

*Scripture*: "It is by grace [God's remarkable compassion and favor drawing you to Christ] that you have been saved [actually delivered from judgment and given eternal life] through faith. And this [salvation] is not of yourselves [not through your own effort], but it is the [undeserved, gracious] gift of God" (Eph. 2:8 AMP).

*Step of faith and obedience*: I won't accept any new leadership positions at church for the rest of the year. Instead, I'll spend extra time and effort asking God to anchor my identity and worth in Him, not in what I do.

*Thank God*: God, I worship You and thank You for firmly rooting my identity in the person of Jesus Christ.

## Relational
*Internal barrier*: Unforgiveness.

*Source*: I had a huge misunderstanding with a man who was vital to our mission, and I am struggling to extend forgiveness.

*Scripture*: "As God's chosen people, holy and dearly loved, clothe yourselves with compassion, kindness, humility, gentleness and patience. Bear with each other and forgive one another if any of you has a grievance against someone. Forgive as the Lord forgave you. And over all these virtues put on love, which binds them all together in perfect unity" (Col. 3:12–14).

*Step of faith and obedience*: I will humble myself and apologize to this person for my part of the breakdown. I'll forgive him and ask for forgiveness.

*Thank God*: Thank You, God, for modeling unconditional love and forgiveness through Your Son.

## Health
*Internal barrier*: Addiction to overeating. I feel that food is the only thing that can fill my need for comfort.

*Source*: When things get stressful, I use food to cope.

*Scripture*: "This is my comfort in my affliction, that Your word has revived me *and* given me life" (Ps. 119:50 AMP).

*Step of faith and obedience*: I will increase my time in God's Word in the evening when I'm tempted to eat for comfort. I'll go for a walk one night a week.

*Thank God*: God, thank You for being my Comforter!

## ADDICTIONS, ABUSE, AND MENTAL ILLNESS

Some deeply rooted strongholds such as substance abuse, addictions, or a history of greedy business practices will require an intense amount of internal work on your part. Chronic sins require deep healing. If you are not achieving a united victory over an internal barrier, you may need additional help. That's okay. Satan will lure you into believing you are the only one who has ever committed your particular sin and that there is no way out of your destructive choices. It's a lie. And with God there is always hope and help!

While your hope is firm and secure in Christ (Heb. 6:19), the help you need may be found in a knowledgeable pastor, counselor, recovery ministry, health-care provider, or other resource. Sometimes talking with another couple who has been through the same thing is the first important step in your united victory.

The serious issue of mental illness should never be overlooked, nor the need for professional intervention. In years past, mental illness was largely neglected by the church. Today, though, thanks to the efforts of nationally recognized leaders such as Rick and Kay Warren and many others, mental illness is finally being addressed within the church, and resources to help those who are dealing with it are being developed within the Christian community.

Unfortunately, much stigma is still attached to mental illness, and controversy continues over how Christians should deal with it, ranging from the use of prescription medications to certain therapeutic models. In general, we wholeheartedly recommend that you unashamedly seek professional help if you experience or encounter mental, emotional, or behavioral patterns that could suggest mental illness. Having dealt with these issues in our own extended family, we are compassionate advocates for those who struggle with mental illness. (See appendix A for a list of resources.)

Whatever their source or circumstance, internal strongholds can annihilate you if left unchecked. For almost a decade, Clint and I lived in personal defeat from past patterns before we believed that, with the hope of Christ and help from others, we could rise out of the deep holes we'd dug for ourselves and leave our shovels behind. You can too.

Even with the enemy's taunts in your ears, hear us cheering you on in your courageous fight for personal and marital wholeness. Remember that your enemies are also God's enemies. And although Satan will stop at nothing to divide you, Jesus Christ likewise stopped at nothing to unite you. At the moment of His death, you were given the spiritual power to surmount or obliterate every type of external or internal barrier set before you. Jesus's death and resurrection flipped off the spiritual switch in the kingdom of hell and eternally ignited the supernatural power of Christ in you. "With God we will gain the victory, and he will trample down our enemies" (Ps. 60:12).

---

## Pray Together

Lord of heaven's armies, we need Your protection against the division caused by external and internal barriers. We believe You have new territory for us to possess, but we need Your power to cross every Jordan and conquer every Jericho. We confess the temptation to turn back or give up when we're hard pressed by trials. Grant us the faith and obedience to advance together, not retreat or split apart. Help us to be victorious over our barriers. Set us free from strongholds of any sort. We know that in Your kingdom, great trials are the means to great triumphs because of Jesus Christ. Let us be willing to seek help where we need it. Your Word is alive, and we believe it holds the power to break through every barrier and tear down every stronghold. In Jesus's mighty name, we come against those things for Your glory. Amen.

---

## Taking the Next Step

Use these questions as discussion points. You may also wish to record some answers or insights in your journal.

1. Your mission to lead in-home Bible studies for new parents starts off with a bang when eight couples come to your house the first night. The next morning, however, your homeowner's association files a grievance against you. They cite your HOA contract, which clearly states that guests to your home must not park on the street and that next time they do so, they will all be cited. Your mission has just hit an external barrier. Using the tools described in this chapter, how will you proceed?

2. Think of at least one external barrier you're experiencing in your marriage right now. Openly discuss your differences. As with the exercise of exposing broken trust in chapter 6, this is not an exercise in fault-finding but in fact-finding. You're trying to learn from each other and honor your differences. You're also allowing the Holy Spirit to reconcile or fuse your differences together through honest dialogue and prayer.

3. Think about each of the seven sectors of marriage and identify one internal barrier (an area of skewed thinking or relating). Follow these steps to draw on your weapons of faith:
   - Name the stronghold.
   - Identify its source.
   - Locate a Scripture verse or passage to pray over your problem.
   - Pray about the steps of obedience and faith God is directing you to take.
   - Thank God for His work on your behalf.

4. Is there any addiction, stronghold, or pattern of behavior in your life that may require additional help from a trained professional or other support provider? Explain your answer. What steps can you take to get the assistance you need?

## Chapter 14

# Sneak Attacks

*You will never glory in God till, first of all, God*
*has killed your glorying in yourself.*
—CHARLES SPURGEON, "Glorying in the Lord"

One of Satan's most effective battle tactics is the sneak attack or ambush—an unexpected assault launched from a hidden place.

When I was fighting overseas, we were taught never to pick up stuff off the ground, no matter how appealing it appeared. "Charlie" was skilled at using inanimate objects as bait. These items were triggered to explode and kill every person in range of the blast. The North Vietnamese also used other booby traps and trip wires invisible to the naked eye.

Satan is no different. He skillfully baits God's people into traps. Second Corinthians 11:14 tells us that Satan "masquerades as an angel of light." J. Vernon McGee expands on the verse: "Satan himself is an angel of *light*. If he would make himself visible to you, you would see breathtaking beauty."[5] Hard to believe but true. And that's not all. Satan not only appears attractive at times, but he is also adept at the art of camouflage, concealing his ugly presence or evil intent in the midst of your natural surroundings.

This chapter will highlight Satan's two most alluring and subtle snares. Both involve pride, and if they go undetected, the resultant explosions will cause extensive casualties.

## THE TRIP WIRE OF "MORE IS BETTER"

Pride can sneak up on you. Expect it. Pride is subtle and subconscious. It often appears as something alluring that plays upon your weaknesses and draws upon your strengths.

For example, Clint and I taught school for a combined total of twenty years. Teaching is wound into the very fabric of our DNA. We'd earned accolades in the educational field and were accustomed to teaching packed classrooms. I had also designed curricula and trained other teachers in and outside our school district. Every workshop I led was well attended. Clint and I assumed all this would transfer over into God's mission for our marriage. Wrong.

Our first marriage workshop contained four people, and one of them was the proctor. We soon discovered this would be the norm, not the exception. There have been (and still are) countless times when we've spoken to a gathering of ten or fewer.

One Friday night we shared our testimony at a small country church in the cornfields of Illinois. Our engagement took place the same evening as a high school football game. Not good. We went to bed assuring ourselves that more people would come the next morning since it wouldn't compete with any sporting events. Instead, even fewer people showed up. Due to the low numbers, we had to completely reconfigure how we presented the material. Our egos required a major readjustment too.

Despite our feelings, God had His own agenda for that weekend. Since there were so few people, we decided to conclude the seminar with a time of intimate sharing and prayer. What transpired never would have happened in a crowd. Raw and tender wounds were exposed. Pain was openly shared. Tears were shed. Burdens released. Prayers offered. Embraces exchanged. The sacred ground we traversed together couldn't be compared to anything else we'd experienced. No matter who did or didn't show up, the Counselor had come.

"Why is it that when only a handful of people attend, we dismiss the value of what God is doing?" Clint wondered. It was a sobering question. In a society that values gains and good stats, over and over we've been bombarded by questions about numbers. "How many marriages have you saved?" "How many percentage points has the divorce rate dropped in the cities where you've served?"

After wrestling at length with why we equated high attendance with effectiveness in ministry, we finally agreed to add the following standard to our marriage mission creed: we will never cancel an event due to a low turnout. Regardless of how many people show up, we'll do what God has called us to do and entrust the outcome to His capable hands. After all, He is the Good Shepherd who leaves the ninety-nine to go after the one: "What do you think? If a man owns a hundred sheep, and one of them wanders away, will he not leave the ninety-nine on the hills and go to look for the one that wandered off? And if he finds it, truly I tell you, he is happier about that one sheep than about the ninety-nine that did not wander off" (Matt. 18:12–13).

Our friends Ben and Jennifer have a mission to teach God's truths to the third and fourth generations of their family. Last summer they organized a camp for their four grandkids. They spent a week using indoor and outdoor activities to teach God's principles. At the end of camp, the parents were invited to watch a video of the adventures and lessons learned together. Does their mission have less value because it touches only a few children? Of course not.

If you knew God's mission for your marriage would make a difference to only one other person, would you still be as passionate about carrying it out? How about five people? Ten?

Our world emphasizes the masses while turning away from the one. Facebook likes, viral videos, and flocks of Twitter followers don't impress God, but they can puff up your ego. Maybe your mission is about investing in a small group of people. Or the spiritual legacy of your immediate family. Having a small number of people impacted by your mission doesn't mean your mission has less worth. That's a trap. Jesus invested in only twelve men, but they turned the world upside down.

## THE TRIP WIRE OF BRIGHT LIGHTS AND BIG CITIES

Many people in pursuit of accomplishing a dream or a mission move from small to big. A singer might say, "I'm famous! For years I performed in all the small venues before hitting the big time. Now I play to sold-out stadiums."

Penny and I got tangled up by this trip wire at the start of our mission. Many of our friends and ministry heroes were speaking in exciting and fancy places. We incorrectly assumed this meant their missions had more value, so we subconsciously began measuring our effectiveness with those same scales. When we were sent as marriage missionaries to the glamourous city of Rome, we felt like we were finally doing something of value.

Then one day, back in the States, we met a woman who owned a pig farm. "Will you come over for some refreshments and a tour of my farm?" Penny and I had just finished a long weekend of teaching, and we looked forward to some down time before our next engagement. However, just before we left the church, the woman approached us with her unique invitation. During our seminar, she had poured out her heart about the pain in her marriage. As we looked into her tired eyes, I knew we couldn't turn her down. If she'd invited us to Paris rather than a pig farm, wouldn't we have jumped at the chance to go?

"I need to warn you. When you go into the barn, the smell will stay on your skin, clothes, and hair." Having lived in Oklahoma for eleven years, I knew what our hostess meant. Not Penny, though. She's a city girl. And although she was exhausted, I knew she wouldn't pass up the chance to take photographs of the newborn piglets. With a camera around her neck, she stepped into a large pair of rubber boots and followed the farmer through the barn door.

The stench was overwhelming. Despite the horrible smell, the squeals and grunts were enough to keep Penny in the barn for a few minutes. The rest of the afternoon was spent walking from barn to barn and story to story. The woman was proud to show us what it took to keep the family farm running. Even if only for a few hours, her loneliness and pain were replaced with the company of two strangers. By the end of the afternoon, her countenance had completely changed. Ours had too.

For several reasons, the impact of this experience lingered much longer than the smell of pigs. God used the farm to remind us that we should never be allured by the booby trap of bright lights, big cities, and all they represent. The pig farm was God's reminder to us that we will always encounter Him most profoundly in the out-of-the-way places. Over and over again, the Bible reflects this same idea. Here is one example: "Now that same day two of them were going to a village called Emmaus, about seven miles from Jerusalem. They were talking with each other about everything that had happened. As they talked and discussed these things with each other, Jesus himself came up and walked along with them; but they were kept from recognizing him" (Luke 24:13–16).

The two disciples in that passage weren't hanging out amongst the hustle and bustle of the city. They were miles away from all that when a third party unexpectedly joined them. Although at first they didn't recognize Jesus, their eyes were eventually opened and their hearts set ablaze: "They asked each other, 'Were not our hearts burning within us while he talked with us on the road and opened the Scriptures to us?'" (Luke 24:32).

That story from the gospel of Luke helped solidify our afternoon on the pig farm. Not until we, like the two disciples walking the Emmaus road, allowed God to take us far from the well-traveled trails and to less enticing places did we encounter Him like never before.

Here are further examples of this principle in the Bible:

- Moses—In the middle of a barren wilderness, he encounters God's presence in a burning bush (Exod. 3:1–5).
- Ezekiel—Exiled at the river Kebar, the prophet receives vivid visions from God (Ezek. 1:1).
- Paul—Blinded on the road to Damascus, the church's persecutor becomes God's powerhouse (Acts 9:1–5).
- Philip—Far beyond Jerusalem, he encounters an unsaved Ethiopian eunuch and baptizes him on the spot (Acts 8:26–40).
- John—Exiled on the island of Patmos, the beloved disciple receives his profound revelation of Jesus Christ (Rev. 1:9).

The Lord Jesus Himself often retreated to lonely and barren places to meet alone with His Father. As seen from the biblical illustrations in this chapter, solitude has always been God's gateway to soul riches—the true treasure of knowing Him. Sometimes God has a work to do in one heart that can't be done in a crowd. When He leads you to an out-of-the-way place or even benches you for a time, be assured that something new will grow in your humble surroundings. New things take time. Stay with Him there until He is done.

 Off the Beaten Path, Pedro and Tania • *5:02 minutes*

## THE BENEFITS OF HUMILITY

As a people, why are we so easily enticed by pride and so resistant to humility? Clint and I define *humility* as that unique place where our nothing meets God's everything. When we humble ourselves before God or He humbles us, a divine exchange takes place. Something in the human heart is transformed for the better. Consider these verses about humility, and note the many blessings and benefits promised to the humble:

- "If my people, who are called by my name, will humble themselves and pray and seek my face and turn from their wicked ways, then I will hear from heaven, and I will forgive their sin and will heal their land" (2 Chron. 7:14).
- "He guides the humble in what is right and teaches them his way" (Ps. 25:9).
- "The LORD sustains the humble but casts the wicked to the ground" (Ps. 147:6).
- "For the LORD takes delight in his people; he crowns the humble with victory" (Ps. 149:4).
- "For those who exalt themselves will be humbled, and those who humble themselves will be exalted" (Matt. 23:12).
- "But he gives us more grace. That is why Scripture says: 'God opposes the proud but shows favor to the humble'" (James 4:6).

Allowing pride to become entangled with any aspect of God's mission is like getting caught in a sneak attack with unlimited trip wires. If one doesn't snag you, another will. How do you untangle yourself?

The best defense against pride is to daily confess your offense(s). Admitting your pride and changing your behavior makes you a more authentic person. How do you confess pride and turn away from it? Let's look at the apostle Paul for a noteworthy how-to example.

No matter how far and wide Paul's ministry spread, he never forgot the mercy and grace of God. He called himself "less than the least of all the Lord's people" (Eph. 3:8). He also referred to himself as having been "a blasphemer and a persecutor and a violent man" (1 Tim. 1:13). As the self-proclaimed vilest offender, Paul openly confessed to being a staunch persecutor of the church and dead set against the cause of Christ. He no longer acted in ways that were unbecoming. Paul never lost sight of whom he'd been and what he'd done before being knocked down by God's blinding light. He kept a humble posture, bowing as a beggar before a king. As Christ-followers we are instructed to do the same.

In *The Solomon Secrets*, Robert Jeffress writes, "Genuine humility is crucial to the successful life." He goes on to say, "Pride is a prerequisite for failure, and humility is a prerequisite for success."[6]

We wrote about the act of humble confession very briefly in chapter 6, but it merits a second look here. Confessing pride and humbling yourself before God and your spouse must become part of the culture of your marriage. By the word *culture*, we mean that humility regularly manifests itself as a part of who you are together. The strongest marriages and most potent missions are those in which both spouses are slow to point the finger at each other and quick to accept responsibility for their own actions.

"I'm sorry. I spoke rudely to you today. Will you forgive me?"

"I was wrong about our discussion."

"I made a huge mistake and I want to tell you what I did."

"I feel really embarrassed about this, but I need to confess that I . . ."

"There's no excuse for what I said. I'm sorry that my words hurt you."

It's easy to grow apathetic about acknowledging pride and to become quick at calling attention to the faults of others. This is especially true in a marriage on God's mission. His mission will press and pinch you. It will sweep you up in its flurry of needs. It will test every ounce of your pride and your patience. Serving side by side is so challenging at times that some couples won't even attempt it.

Perhaps it's only natural to direct your frustrations toward your spouse, but that doesn't mean it's okay. Sometimes Penny and I confess our sins while praying with each other. Sometimes we do it during our time together on Sunday nights. Whatever the case, confession always includes apologies, forgiveness, and grace, but we had to learn how to do those things by practicing them. God has examined and humbled us up one side and down the other, and He isn't done yet.

Confess your pride to God as soon as He brings it to your attention. Even better, do so aloud. If you need to, also confess it to your spouse or a trusted friend. Most people didn't grow up with a model of relational humility, so it takes practice and grace to get to where you can willingly and regularly be real and vulnerable before God and each other.

Every marriage has disagreeable days when it's so very tempting to throw each other under the tank. But doing so dishonors God. Instead of looking for ways to sabotage each other, what would happen if you chose to watch each other's back? Covering each other in love is the biblical response God desires for His people. "Above all, love each other deeply, because love covers over a multitude of sins" (1 Peter 4:8).

---

## Pray Together

Father, we humbly confess the sin of pride. Forgive us for the thoughts and behaviors we've exhibited that don't please You and for the times we've measured our effectiveness by the world's standards. Keep us far from the sneak attacks and hidden traps of pride.

May we be a people who repent of our bent toward mega-everything. Make us content in You alone, no matter how things add up.

Father, You accomplished some of Your most miraculous work in the lives of those who were not living within the bustle of the world. You chose faraway places to make Yourself known. Grant us the self-discipline to take advantage of alone time instead of filling it with busyness and activity. May our mission be one that exhibits humility at all times in all ways. In Jesus's name. Amen.

---

### Taking the Next Step

Use these questions as discussion points. You may also wish to record some answers or insights in your journal.

1. Talk honestly about any struggles you've experienced with numbers or statistics. For example, are you shooting for a certain number of people to impact? How have you used a measuring stick for your mission that isn't like God's?
2. Describe a time when you took a less traveled road (literally or figuratively). How did that experience impact you?
3. Take some time to write a note of encouragement to one person. Personalize it by writing it in your own handwriting and snail-mailing it. No texts or emails allowed.
4. Is there anything you need to confess before God and your spouse? If so, do it now. Don't wait.

## Chapter 15

# Incoming!

*We are not "born again" into soft and protected nurseries,*
*but into open country where we suck strength from the*
*very terror of the tempest.*
—JOHN HENRY JOWETT, "The Price of Liberty"

During my duty as a military policeman, the initial hardships—homesickness, bossy sergeants, dirt, monsoons, snakes, gnats, ticks, mosquitoes, and leeches—gave way to intense tragedies such as losing a fellow soldier in combat. As I witnessed more casualties, my perception of "hardships" changed. At times I questioned what I was even doing in Vietnam and whether or not I'd make it out alive. When I finally did, I wanted no part of guns, ammo, or anything else that had to do with war.

Until Penny and I started our mission to reconcile and strengthen marriages, I thought I was done with enemy fire. But our solo mission trip to Greece and Israel brought back memories of the war. On our first day in Athens, political protest quickly grew unruly, and gunfire erupted in the streets. All access to our hotel by car was blocked. As shots were fired, we unloaded our gear from the rental car and carried it through the darkened streets toward our hotel. The gunfire and our tour guide's instructions left us shell-shocked.

"Wait a few hours for the shooting to stop and then walk back to get your car." Besides the danger involved, Penny and I weren't even sure we could find the car again.

The incident in Athens was not our only near miss on that trip. A week later, while we were driving from Jericho to Jerusalem, an explosion rocked our rental van. When the second blast sounded, traffic came to a halt and police blocked off the road. Plumes of smoke billowed into the sky about a quarter of a mile ahead. Explosions three, four, and five were so powerful that the concussions rattled our ribcages. As soon as the bombing stopped, we hightailed it to our hotel in Jerusalem, filled with doubt and fear. Questions crept in as we processed what had just happened. *Had we not heard God right about going on this trip to serve Him overseas? Why was He allowing us to be in such danger? Were we not where God wanted us to be?*

While you probably won't experience a literal artillery attack as we did, your own mission will come under heavy fire. At times the difficulties will trigger fear, doubt, and disappointment. Questions will swirl and surface: *Did we really hear from God regarding His mission for our marriage? Did we do something wrong? Why hasn't God answered our prayers?*

Delays, Questions, and Struggles, Dennis and Denise •
*3:59 minutes*

Delays, Questions, and Struggles, David and Cindy •
*2:25 minutes*

Delays, Questions, and Struggles, Rob and Panda •
*7:01 minutes*

## GOD VALUES SUFFERING

Grief. Pain. Suffering. No one likes to talk about *that* part of God's mission. We don't either. But over the years, we've sat across from too many couples who were desperately scrambling to pick up the pieces of their crumbled marriages and missions because they did not know how to suffer together. Instead, their suffering blew them apart. They possessed no long-term plan of defense to combat the pain.

In *The Fire of Delayed Answers*, Bob Sorge writes, "In the face of delayed answers, it takes great faith to persevere in seeking only the face of God—to 'cry out day and night to Him.' Because your mind will imagine all kinds of other possible sources of relief you could conceivably pursue."[7]

It could be financial reprieve for which you long, or the return of a wandering loved one. Perhaps you continue to pray for the restoration of a broken relationship or the physical healing of a friend. Maybe you're feeling confused, exhausted, burned out, disillusioned, or all of the above. Severe trials strike against the very structure of your relationship. Even when you know God is able to bring good from what feels so very terrible, the pain and grief of the present override your ability to care about the future. You seek a prescription for your pain, and there is none. Despite how much you pray, circumstances seem to get worse instead of better, threatening to blow you up with the force of a grenade.

The church can paint a skewed picture of Christianity, glossing over the fact that we'll experience terrible pain on this side of heaven.

But Jesus stated otherwise: "Here on earth you will have many trials and sorrows" (John 16:33 NLT).

God's mission for your marriage isn't for wimps. Satan loves it when we raise a white flag during times of affliction. That is always his highest aim. So a tough season means you must stand firmly upon this truth: suffering is a hallmark of all God's chosen people.

Many Old Testament prophets suffered severe loss and pain. These individuals tried tirelessly to carry out the missions God had given them, warning the Israelites of imminent destruction if they continued in sin. The prophets listened to God's voice and did exactly what He asked of them, often serving as a literal symbol of the message they heralded. And they suffered. Repeatedly.

So allow us to pose a question: Do you know how to suffer *together*? Do you know how to keep your marriage united, or even make it stronger, when something horrible unexpectedly sweeps through your lives—and doesn't go away?

We ask you these questions because no one asked them of us, and we wish they would have.

In the winter of 2011, our lives blew into a billion tiny pieces with one phone call. I (Penny) could hardly make sense of my sister's sobs and screams over the phone as she cried out my name. It took several moments to figure out what she was trying to say before I collapsed. Our younger brother had ended his brave twenty-year battle with mental illness by barricading himself in his bedroom and taking his own life. I remember crumpling into a ball on the carpet. Clint got down on the floor next to me and held me as I wailed, overcome by a cruel and crippling sorrow. This would be our entry into the hallowed halls of prolonged suffering.

We had never learned how to suffer *together* as a couple. It would take several weeks for the shock of Jay's suicide to wear off and reality to kick in. Unbeknownst to us at the time, everything regarding our marriage and God's mission would be changed forever. Traumatic loss does that.

Loss of any kind packs tremendous potential for marital division, and Satan seems to especially target husbands and wives who are serving God. Whether it's the death of a loved one, job loss, depression, disillusionment, or some other struggle you're experiencing or will experience, learning to suffer together means intentionally training your spirits to follow hard after God and learning to see Him in the middle of life's most tragic moments. But how?

## RESPECT EACH OTHER'S GRIEVING PROCESS

Men and women experience and express sorrow and grief in drastically different ways, but you can learn how to respect each other's needs. After we lost Penny's brother, I got out all my Super 8 film reels from Vietnam and watched them over and over again. I don't fully understand why I had that need, but I did. In addition, I regrieved the loss of my dad, which had happened when I was in Nam. Penny didn't share this same manner of grieving, but she honored what I needed to do by asking questions about what I was doing and how I felt. She valued my actions even though she didn't understand them.

Penny, on the other hand, cried more often and more deeply than I'd ever seen her cry before. Eventually she began using visual arts to outwardly express her pain. Attending various grief groups also became important to her healing. For several months she went to a grief counselor. I didn't share those same needs, nor did I understand them. However, I gave her the freedom to grieve and heal in her own way. When she invited me to attend grief meetings for spouses and support providers, I participated to learn more about what she was experiencing. I also filmed and edited a video testimonial for her hospice counselors. In this way I could give something back to the people who were giving so much support to my wife.

Because men and women grieve differently, try to find at least one new thing you can share together through the sorrow. One unexpected way we grieved together was watching emotionally charged movies. These movies, which depicted stories of hardships, gave us a way to learn something together from the characters, discuss our different responses, and process our own feelings about how those things related to our grief.

The ways you and your spouse express loss are unique to your personalities; allow each other that uniqueness. There are no exact steps for healing, nor is there a timeline; however, studying each other's needs and validating each other's expressions of pain can make all the difference. Learn as much as you can about the attributes of grief, such as depression, lethargy, confusion, flashbacks, anger, regret, and fear. Be a student of your suffering and that of your spouse. In this way, you take an active part in your healing as well as his or hers. (For those who have experienced loss and are struggling, a list of recommended resources can be found in appendix B.)

## CRAWL BACK INTO THE BUNKER

During the war, bunkers provided safe, reinforced below-ground shelters for us GIs. In them we sought protection from danger as well as medical assistance, help from our commanding officers, and connection with our fellow soldiers.

When you go through difficult times, you need that same type of safe shelter—a protected space where you can step away from the chaos of your surroundings and just be with God. You are broken, and it takes time and effort to heal.

Despite all that God had brought Penny and me through in the past, we were extremely naive about the ways grief would drastically alter the landscape of our lives. With much intention, we crawled back into the bunker of our home for refuge. This included shutting down all active forms of God's mission for several months. We also increased our time with Him and read a lot about grief to try to understand what the journey of loss entailed. Listening to old hymns and reading the book of Psalms were steady sources of comfort.

In times of loss and suffering, you may find it challenging to pray, especially together. But prayer is essential. It's our direct line to our Commanding Officer—the One who sees the entire battle. One helpful suggestion is to use short, one- or two-sentence prayers that you can repeat as needed. Here are some examples:

- God, how do we cope with this great loss? Speak to us through Your Word and Your Holy Spirit. We need Your comfort and peace.
- Fill the immense void in our hearts with more of Your truth, hope, and love.
- Help us to bring all our losses before You, Jesus. Fill us with the confidence that You will receive our pain at the cross and heal us.
- Jesus, You are the only one who knows and understands our pain. Please do not let it divide us, but through it let us unite together.
- Please lead us to the passages in Your Word, to other biblical resources, and to people who can help us express our grief in constructive and meaningful ways.
- God, we don't want to become hardened, sarcastic, cynical, or edgy toward each other because of this grief. Keep our hearts tender.
- Lord, we give You all the things that are making us feel chaotic, afraid, stressed, and anxious. We set each of these feelings down before You and ask for Your help and healing.
- Examine our hearts, Lord. Show us what You see when You look inside our sadness and pain. Help us not give way to depression and despair.

Whether you need some basic first aid or extended time in the infirmary, God always desires your personal wholeness and healing.

Remember your three main weapons as a soldier? The Bible, prayer, and worship are your direct path to healing all wounds, whatever their cause. Using them consistently may be a struggle, and there will be times when you need the Holy Spirit to take your groans and intercede for you (Rom. 8:26). This is absolutely understandable. Allow yourself the time and safe space you need, without feeling rushed or selfish.

## DEVELOP YOUR NIGHT VISION

For better visibility at night, the army used something called a Starlight scope. In the dark, it could help me see what my naked eyes could not. But not every soldier carried his own scope. Therefore, we were also taught how to increase our night vision by covering our eyes for ten seconds and then uncovering them. We practiced how to see well in the dark. When I arrived in Vietnam, I understood why we practiced this skill so often. The nights were blacker than black.

As the body of Christ prepares for His return, tragedies and troubles will only continue to increase in scope and sequence. You must train your eyes to see in this dark world, when all goodness and light have been extinguished. One way to develop spiritual night vision is to study other people in the Bible who have gone through terrible ordeals. The book of Job has much to say about tragedy and man's response to it. The book of Lamentations contains exactly what its title denotes: a perpetual cry. Many of the psalms also express life's sorrows and proclaim God's comfort.

You may also know people in your church who have lived through some hard circumstances. Ask them how they survived. Be a student of their suffering. How did they make it through their hardship, and how did they allow what happened to change them?

Another helpful tool to learn how to endure hard times is to make a set of "night vision Scripture cards"—that is, copy comforting verses from the Bible onto index cards. Using a concordance in the back of your Bible or an online Bible search engine, look up key-words such as *tragedy, help, tears, cry, comfort, grief, peace,* and *hope* and then look through the verses listed under those words. Write the verses you find most meaningful onto index cards that you keep with you at all times. Read them silently. Read them aloud. Pray them often. Claim every verse as God's personal promise for you. For starters, here are some suggestions:

- "The LORD is close to the brokenhearted" (Ps. 34:18).
- "Blessed are the poor in spirit, for theirs is the kingdom of heaven. Blessed are those who mourn, for they will be comforted" (Matt. 5:3-4).
- "Our light and momentary troubles are achieving for us an eternal glory that far outweighs them all" (2 Cor. 4:17).
- "Be of good courage, and He shall strengthen your heart, all you who hope in the LORD" (Ps. 31:24 NKJV).
- "You have been a shelter for me, a strong tower from the enemy. I will abide in Your tabernacle forever; I will trust in the shelter of Your wings" (Ps. 61:3-4 NKJV).

My unit in Vietnam was often assigned to pull night security on firebase camps to which we traveled. When we heard the enemy approaching, my job was to shoot up a flare to illuminate the darkness. Your flare is the Word of God. The Bible says, "Your word is a lamp for my feet, a light on my path" (Ps. 119:105). Your night vision Scripture cards will shed the light you need when darkness rolls in. Because God's Word is alive (Heb. 4:12), it has the power to breathe life into all your dead and dying places.

The Grief of God's Mission, Larry and Carrie • *3:54 minutes*

## SUFFERING AND YOUR SEVEN MARRIAGE SECTORS

Suffering can significantly impact and change your marriage in all seven sectors. Allow us to give you an example from a couple we met. David and Beth are currently facing a hardship involving addiction. The scope of what has happened to their family has knocked them down spiritually. Hope is running out. No matter how much they pray, nothing seems to change. Many extended family relationships have deteriorated because of what has happened. Fights and squabbles back and forth are splitting family members into separate camps. The couple's increased financial needs and the legal system have sucked down their bank account. Both are under enormous stress, and various illnesses have ravaged their health. Neither of them is able to work. Their home has become a place of chaos and strife.

Given all these factors, David and Beth understandably have no energy left to dream with God. All seven sectors of their marriage have been impacted by one horrible trial.

Think about a hardship you've gone through or are going through right now. Or think of a couple you're close to who is facing a heartbreaking circumstance. Can you detect the ways in which the hardship is impacting all seven sectors of marriage?

Whether suffering impacts all or even just a few of your seven marriage sectors, it's easy to become discouraged, especially regarding God's mission. Part of that discouragement comes from trying to reconcile yourselves to experiencing tragedy and pain right smack-dab in the center of God's will.

In his classic collection on prayer, E. M. Bounds penned the following: "In the New Testament there are three words used that embrace trouble: *tribulation, suffering,* and *affliction.* The words differ somewhat, but each of them means 'trouble' of some kind. . . . When confirming the souls of the saints and exhorting them to continue in the faith, [Paul] told them, 'we must through much tribulation enter into the kingdom of God' [Acts 14:22]. He knew this by his own experience, for his pathway was anything but smooth and flowery."[8]

When you suffer inside of God's will, you must know beyond all knowing that tribulation does *not* mean you're headed in the wrong direction. Quite the opposite is true. When you fully believe in the promises of His Word and in the faithful God who made them, your tragedies will always carry within them His redemptive plan.

Every last shred of suffering you'll experience will be met by a greater measure of God's presence. But you have to look for Him— sometimes looking hard. Doing so doesn't come naturally. Finding God in the midst of great tragedy is a supernatural experience made possible by the Holy Spirit. Ask Him for help. Make a daily list of the ways you see God show up. Your flesh will fight to focus on the trauma, grief, and loss. There will be days when you want to pack up your mission marbles and go home. And while it may sound as if we're not ending this chapter on a high note, remember: *this is not the end.* Jesus said we would have trouble, but that isn't His final word on the matter. This is: "Take heart! I have overcome the world" (John 16:33).

No matter what you experience in your marriage, the one thing you can count on is the only thing you need: God. His track record in times of tragedy will always prove that you can put all your eggs in that one basket called *grace,* the focus of the next chapter.

---

## Pray Together

Heavenly Father, we trust Your sovereign hand in our suffering. Jesus is the model we must follow when we're faced with trials, and the cross is the only place for our pain. Give us the courage to lay our sorrow before You and ask for help, hope, and healing. We don't like pain, especially when we can't understand the reason certain things happen. In those moments, give us the compassion and consolation we need to believe You and trust Your promises.

In times of loss, each of us grieves differently. We need Your comfort to sustain us. Show us how to seek You for peace and let Your Holy Spirit meet our emotional needs. Don't let us hide or stuff our feelings but, rather, honestly cry them out. When our hearts are broken, bind up our wounds.

Show us how to study each other's grief. Don't let the enemy separate us in times of hardship. Anchor our suffering in Your Word, and provide the truths we need to confront and endure the pain. In troublesome times, may we honor You and give You glory. In Jesus's name we pray. Amen.

---

## Taking the Next Step

Use these questions as discussion points. You may also wish to record some answers or insights in your journal.

1. What have been the most significant losses in your life? In your marriage? How have you responded to those losses, whether positively or negatively?
2. If you've experienced suffering and loss as a couple, how has it changed your marriage? Discuss both the negative and the positive outcomes. (Spouses often differ as to what they consider loss. There are no right or wrong answers.)
3. Look up the passages listed below and write down the benefits, blessings, and promises of tribulation. Then compare your notes with each other.

   Husbands, look up:
   - Romans 5:1–5
   - Romans 8:18–30
   - 2 Corinthians 1:3–11

Wives, look up:
- 2 Thessalonians 1:3–12
- James 5:7–11
- 1 Peter 4:12–19

4. In what ways do the two of you grieve differently? In what ways do you grieve similarly?

## Chapter 16

# The Beauty of Battle Scars

*Suffering, failure, loneliness, sorrow,*
*discouragement, and death will be part of your journey,*
*but the kingdom of God will conquer all these horrors.*
*No evil can resist grace forever.*
—BRENNAN MANNING, *The Ragamuffin Gospel*

During my time in Vietnam, it was easy for me to detect the more seasoned veterans of combat. Their battle scars gave them away. We called them lifers: men and women wholly committed to serving their country for the rest of their lives, no matter the intensity of the fight or how deep their wounds.

Physically speaking, a scar is the result of the body's natural healing process, when fibrous tissue replaces normal skin after injury. While a scar indicates you've been injured, it also shows you've been healed.

If you haven't been wounded already, you will be. But God's grace (undeserved favor) will transform your wounds into scars—indicators of both your injury and of God's healing in your life. The grief of God's mission will always be redeemed by the grace of God. And that grace turns your battle scars into beauty marks. In the words of the Christian classic *Streams in the Desert*, "It is from suffering that the strongest souls ever known have emerged; the world's greatest display of character is seen in those who exhibit the scars of sorrow; the martyrs of the ages have worn their coronation robes that have glistened with fire, yet through their tears and sorrow have seen the gates of heaven."[9]

## GRACE AS SALVE FOR EACH OTHER

Have you ever looked at a fresh wound? It's not pretty. When Clint had lumbar fusion surgery in 2014, I had to inspect, clean, and dress his incision every day for several weeks, placing ointment on it as needed. I hoped that what I was doing would promote healing.

Like applying salve to a wound, extending grace to your spouse in times of suffering aids in the healing process. In that way, your marriage grows stronger instead of pulling apart due to the struggle. The wound may be temporarily ugly and painful, but salving it with grace will be eternally profitable.

Learning how to extend and apply grace to each other is the means by which unity and intimacy are unearthed and cultivated at the very source of the pain. For example, there were times when I (Clint) couldn't understand why Penny's grief seemed to be changing her so drastically. But God continued to remind me that my job was to pray and extend more and more of His grace to her and to be patient. He urged me to validate her feelings and to pray for her more. Her brother's death sliced her wide open, and my job was to apply grace to that gaping wound each day. This was not a grace I could muster on my own. It had to come from God, and it did. "Let us then approach God's throne of grace with confidence, so that we may receive mercy and find grace to help us in our time of need" (Heb. 4:16).

Every morning when I met alone with God, it was as if He handed me a vessel of His grace and showed me how to pour it over Penny's pain, whenever and wherever it was needed. Even so, I didn't always get it right.

As a man, I found it difficult not to be able to fix or remove Penny's grief. On one evening in particular, I heard her sobbing uncontrollably by the side of our bed. Although she was trying to muffle the sound of her sorrow with a towel, it resounded throughout the whole house. Out of weariness and impatience, I made the mistake of giving way to my old tough-guy approach.

"What's the matter? Why are you crying so hard?" I asked abruptly.

Penny has learned to extend and apply grace to me too in such moments. I know it was tempting for her to unleash all her sadness and pain on me, and to be angry at me for not understanding how she felt. She had every right to fire off at me for being impatient and insensitive, but she didn't. That was grace.

Extending and applying grace goes against our natural tendencies. That night when I (Penny) was crying beside our bed, I wanted to emotionally unload on Clint. I was hurting, exhausted, grief-stricken, and inconsolable. What he said did not meet any of my emotional needs. But I didn't want to add insult to injury, as the saying goes. That would only increase the size of the wound instead of adding a healing touch, and it would stop me from going to the One who could truly heal me.

Your spouse cannot meet your every emotional need in times of sorrow; only God can. He will do something new in your marriage right in the middle of all the mess. It feels as if He is pulling your marriage through a very small knothole in a fence. Grace is the grease that will get you both to the other side together.

Not only do you have to learn to extend grace to each other in marriage but it must be extended in your mission as well. Perhaps after a loss or trial, you are ready to get things moving again. But your spouse isn't ready. Grace helps you wait on your spouse patiently and prayerfully.

God's grace will enable you not only to survive times of tribulation, but to *steward* your suffering together for redemptive purposes in the lives of others. Your battle scars are worth something, and you are responsible for cultivating their potential. If God has entrusted you to suffer, His grace will help you bring forth good out of your pain, whether through a witness to others or by deepening your relationship with your spouse. The very trials that scar you may also take God's mission in a new direction, or augment it in some way.

Talking About Tribulation, Bill and Deb • *5:28 minutes*

## GRACE AS SALVE FOR OTHERS

In the first few weeks after my brother's suicide, people told us that good things would come from our loss and that God would use it to help others. Their words were meant to be comforting, but the grief was far too fresh to find solace in them. Our hearts were torn open and bleeding. The scar hadn't formed yet.

Now, much later, we can see exceptional things that have come through what happened, such as our opening a local center to minister to those who are grieving or experiencing difficulty in their marriage. Opening the ministry center could not have come from anything we did but only by God's application of grace to our wounds.

With God, the darkened tunnel of your greatest sorrow can become the very passageway of your greatest hope. Yes, some days that painful wound can burn a hole clean through the center of your chest. Yet the light of Christ will blaze right through that very painful place, creating a habitat for hope to take root and grow.

In this way, God's grace transforms you from the walking wounded to a wounded warrior, a person who has thrived in battle and who makes his or her wounds available to others as a source of healing. You become a lifer, wholly committed to the mission for life, regardless of the obstacles or pain. Albeit bruised and bloody, this is the beauty of ruin.

As a wounded warrior, you do not hide your scars. You expose them. Jesus so beautifully modeled this principle when, after His death and resurrection, He invited Thomas to reach out and touch the places where the nails had pierced Him (John 20:27). In allowing others to see and reach into and touch your scars, you show that you have suffered long together and lived to tell about it. In this way, your suffering is no longer a hazard but a hallmark, something signifying a holy purity and sacred anointing to serve others.

Did you catch that? Suffering indicates anointing. One of the rarest and costliest commodities in ancient times, used for anointing, was the oil of myrrh, which appears throughout Scripture. This special oil was extracted from the leaves and stems of a small, thorny shrub. To increase the flow of myrrh, the bush was beaten or slashed. Then the myrrh flowed forth in great quantity. While its fragrance was delightful, myrrh was bitter and pungent to the taste.

Myrrh was brought to Jesus at His birth (Matt. 2:11) and applied to His body after death (John 19:39–40). It was also mixed with wine for medicinal purposes (Mark 15:23). But what brings a grief-stricken believer great hope in the midst of all hurt is found in a passage from the Old Testament. In it, God gives Moses the holy recipe to make the highly coveted anointing oil for the priests in the temple.

> Then the LORD said to Moses, "Take the following fine spices: 500 shekels of *liquid myrrh*, half as much (that is, 250 shekels) of fragrant cinnamon, 250 shekels of fragrant calamus, 500 shekels of cassia—all according to the sanctuary shekel—and a hin of olive oil. *Make these into a sacred anointing oil*, a fragrant blend, the work of a perfumer. It will be the

sacred anointing oil. Then use it to anoint the tent of meeting, the ark of the covenant law, the table and all its articles, the lampstand and its accessories, the altar of incense, the altar of burnt offering and all its utensils, and the basin with its stand. You shall consecrate them so they will be most holy, and whatever touches them will be holy.

"Anoint Aaron and his sons and consecrate them so they may serve me as priests. Say to the Israelites, 'This is to be my sacred anointing oil for the generations to come. Do not pour it on anyone else's body and do not make any other oil using the same formula. It is sacred, and you are to consider it sacred. Whoever makes perfume like it and puts it on anyone other than a priest must be cut off from their people.'" (Exod. 30:22–33, italics added)

Generous portions of myrrh were used to make the sacred anointing oil for the temple articles and priests. But how does that apply to you? Much as you may not like your pain, God will anoint you with it if you will let Him.

No one likes to be the myrrh shrub, beaten and slashed. But as you search God's Word, you'll find absolutely no evidence that suffering is supposed to make you give up on God or His mission. The apostle Paul spoke vividly about the trials of his assignment, but he never backed off from what God called and created him to do. Never. "Now I want you to know, brothers and sisters, that what has happened to me has actually served to advance the gospel" (Phil. 1:12). Paul used his troubles to propel God's purposes.

Having said all that, remember that suffering doesn't only have value because something good comes forth from it. Suffering has value because God has ordained it. As you intentionally choose to believe that God will anoint you in and through affliction, you and your spouse will find the hope and strength to carry on together.

And from the very place of your most crushing pain, a sacred fragrance will arise.

For Those Who Weep, Penny ◆ *7:35 minutes*

---

## Pray Together

Heavenly Father, we need Your grace in our suffering. Whether now or in the future, give us spiritual eyes to see Your provision of grace in our circumstances, and let us pour out that grace on each other. Even though we know that suffering is a part of life, we wrestle with the reality of it. Jesus, You modeled a willingness to drink from the Father's cup of suffering, served inside His will. May You be our example in all things. There is always a temptation to shrink back when we face loss. Our flesh recoils and self-protects. Fill us with Your courage and use our adversities to draw us closer to You.

Let Your sacred anointing oil of myrrh pour forth from our scars. May the crushing we must bear release a fragrant aroma for others. In Jesus's name. Amen.

---

## Taking the Next Step

Use these questions as discussion points. You may also wish to record some answers or insights in your journal.

1. How have you experienced God's grace in places of pain?
2. What are some tangible ways you can extend grace to your spouse in times of suffering? Ask your spouse what he or she needs most when harsh trials hit.

3. Have you experienced purpose born from pain, or do you know
   someone who went through something painful and is now using
   their experience to help others? Explain your answer.

*Phase V*

# CHECKPOINTS AND CHARGES

## Chapter 17

# Patrolling Your Borders

*There is no question that we must do more
to secure our borders but how we go about
securing them is also important.*
—MARK UDALL, May 16, 2006

When Clint and I visited Israel, we witnessed many garrison units stationed to defend specified Israeli zones, such as the disputed territories of the West Bank, from combatants. Crossing over into these zones, we were forced to stop at military checkpoints. Armed guards requested our passports and the purpose of our travels while visually scanning the van. Especially sobering was the presence of at least one guard positioned in an open-sided tower. In his or her hands was a semiautomatic rifle locked, loaded, and pointed to fire—finger on the trigger—should an enemy approach.

While God's mission will include hardship and trouble, you will also intersect with "mission garrisons" who will keep watch over you, protect your integrity, and encourage you onward. By definition, a *garrison* denotes a collective body of troops stationed at a particular location to guard it. Sometimes a garrison can also be a home base, such as a fort, castle, or city. For the purposes of this chapter, however, let's define mission garrisons as Christian people or couples who surround your mission and keep it from enemy infiltration. You may meet your garrisons at church or in an organization to which you belong. Perhaps you'll intersect through mutual friends, a city-wide prayer event, or a Christian conference. God will bring others into your life to passionately guard His mission for your marriage. You need them, and in many cases, they need you too.

Throughout the Bible, God's people didn't carry out their missions alone. The apostle Paul is a perfect example of interdependence between God's people. While constantly up against foes who sought to derail his mission, he was also surrounded by believers, like Priscilla and Aquila, who became an integral part of his work (Acts 18). Throughout the New Testament, there is much evidence of the ways God used others to watch over Paul, pray for him, provide for his needs, travel alongside him, and help spread the gospel.

But Paul is hardly the only biblical character blessed with the assistance of a garrison.

- Moses and Zipporah's mission garrison was Jethro, Zipporah's father.
- Esther's mission garrison was Mordecai, her uncle.
- Boaz and Ruth's mission garrison was Naomi, Ruth's mother-in-law.
- David's mission garrison was Jonathan, King Saul's son.
- Elisha's mission garrison was Elijah, his mentor.
- Joseph and Mary's mission garrison was Zechariah and Elizabeth, Mary's cousins.

Here are just some of the many ways a person or couple might serve as a garrison for your mission.

- Garrisons keep your actions aligned with your mission statement. It's easy to get offtrack or lose sight of the main goal or purpose of your mission. You need people who know what God has assigned to you and who will regularly check in with you to be sure you are staying focused.

• Garrisons keep you faithful to your marriage mission creed. You need people who have a copy of your creed and who will hold you to every statement of it. The word used in many Christian circles is *accountability*: answering to God and others. These people are concerned not only about what you do, but also about what you're not doing.

• Garrisons connect you with others. Your mission thrives on people. You need people who will introduce you to others. These new acquaintances will impact your mission and be impacted by it.

• Garrisons encourage and motivate you. God has gifted certain people as encouragers and cheerleaders. Especially when you hit hard times, you will need others to help pick you up, dust you off, and tell you to keep going.

• Garrisons keep you faithful to God's commands. Your mission will be carried out in a world full of evil practices. You need people who will "inspect" your personal lives to look for areas of sin and compromise. These people are not afraid to call you out on your stuff and ask hard questions.

• Garrisons pray for you. Your mission needs to be saturated with prayer. We suggest establishing a prayer team for your marriage and your mission.

• Garrisons brainstorm ideas with you. New challenges will arise, and you need people who will help you generate effective solutions.

• Garrisons provide surveillance over the health of your marriage and family.

• Garrisons serve in your mission. More hands for the harvest are always needed. Physically, you can't do everything. People

with the gift of helps are everywhere, looking for opportunities
to be plugged into work that has value.

• Garrisons are a mouthpiece for your mission. You need people
  who will share your mission with others in positive ways.

• Garrisons are mentors for your mission. There are wise, experienced people who will take you under their guidance and offer
  you solid counsel.

• Garrisons donate to your mission. Most missions require some
  type of funding or at least some supplies. You need faithful
  donors.

• Garrisons open doors for you. Don't think of these people as
  those with power and influence. They can consist of anyone
  through whom God imparts favor.

When Clint and I first started moving forward with God's mission
for our marriage, we felt very alone. Through a variety of circumstances, we met Joe and Michelle Williams, a couple who graciously
became our mission mentors. Having been in marriage ministry for
years, they graciously offered us the wisdom and counsel we needed.
They took an interest in our mission. They also included our story
in their book *Yes, Your Marriage Can Be Saved: 12 Truths for Rescuing
Your Relationship*.

"You must stay focused on *God's* mission—not yours or anyone
else's," Joe said during one of our many meetings. "People will try to
pull you away from it. Their ideas will sound really good. But that
doesn't mean you're supposed to carry them out. Be a spearhead,
not a net. Stick to your mission and don't get sidetracked."

Joe's words still resonate. "Be a spearhead, not a net." We often
visualize him placing his fingertips together to form a point as he
lovingly admonished us to stay focused—doing what we're called to
do, not catching every other idea along the way.

Eventually, God began leading us into relationships with several other couples. Dale and Colleen kept us faithful to the Bible and each other. Don and Kathy were our brainstorming buddies. Gary and Mona kept us sane. Johnathan and Penny prayed for us. Dave and Dawn encouraged us onward. Eric and Jennifer opened ministry doors. Richard and Sharon funded us generously. Ben and Jennifer provided safe shelter. Each of these couples served a different purpose. All of them were needed. Some of them filled more than one role. Over time, they all combined to serve as the collective body of troops stationed to guard God's mission for our marriage. We did the same for them. At the onset, we had no idea we would need others in our lives to fill these roles. Now we cannot imagine our mission without them.

## REGULAR INSPECTIONS

In ancient times, when soldiers returned from battle, they were inspected by their commander in chief or king. A wise leader always knew the condition of his troops.

Because marriages are constantly under fire from Satan, it's critical that you include garrisons who will regularly and honestly inspect your marriage for division or hot spots. Your marriage must stay on track with God. You must stay on track with God. Breaking ranks or going AWOL should never be an option.

Marriages are crumbling at an alarming rate, including those of lay leaders and pastors. No marriage is safe. That includes ours. That includes yours. The main problem is unfaithfulness, which today takes on more forms than ever. In the pre-Internet era, engaging in an extramarital relationship required one person to be in the physical presence of another. No more, though; the Internet and mobile technology put us all just a click away from doing something that displeases God and dishonors our marriage.

Unfaithfulness constitutes the emotional or physical engagement of a spouse in any intimate relationship (in person or via the

Internet, phone, etc.) that invades the bonds of marriage. Emotional affairs, although they may not include direct physical contact, are affairs nonetheless. Why? Because they invade the intimate space solely reserved for our spouse within the bond of marriage.

Given the reality of our human nature, we suggest that you put people in your lives to hold the attitudes, thoughts, and actions in your marriage accountable to God's Word. A prayer partner is ideal. Clint has a married male prayer partner and I have a married female prayer partner. Our prayer partners know our vulnerabilities, temptations, and weaknesses, and they aren't afraid to engage us in courageous conversations. They keep us humble by asking questions we don't want to be asked and noticing things we wish they didn't. We give these people carte blanche to speak into our marriage, and they do the same with us as well.

A prayer-partner relationship operates by the following agreements:

- *Meet together weekly.* We suggest that you connect with your prayer partner at the same day and time each week, preferably face-to-face. For caregivers or parents of small children, tweak this to fit your schedule and the demands on your time.
- *Talk about concerns/struggles.* Your prayer partner is an objective sounding board and an advocate for your marriage.
- *Maintain confidentiality.* Barring a life-threatening circumstance, what each of you shares must stay between the two of you.
- *Pray together.* Share prayer requests that affect your marriage and pray together.
- *Ask tough questions.* There must be freedom to ask questions that feel awkward or uncomfortable. Here are some examples:
    Do you feel drawn to anyone other than your spouse?
    Are you and your spouse spending quality time together?
    Are you hiding anything from your spouse?

Is there a sexual temptation you're struggling with?

Have you emotionally bonded with someone outside your marriage?

* *Disclose temptations and weaknesses.* Confess what needs to be confessed. Be vulnerable enough to admit your temptations in any of the seven sectors of marriage.
* *Hold each other accountable.* Your marriage vows, your marriage mission creed, and God's Word are your plumb line.
* *Celebrate successes.* Witnessing God's activity in your lives is a way to give Him the praise and honor He is due.
* *Mourn losses.* As discussed earlier in the book, grief, loss, and disappointment are some of the most difficult aspects of your lives here on earth. You need someone you can be real with in regard to your personal grief and pain.

## SEARCH AND SWEEP

During combat, sometimes fellow soldiers and I were ordered to conduct a *sweep*—a comprehensive search of an area. Our purpose was to spot and stop enemy infiltration. Sweeps were performed by spacing soldiers some distance apart from each other and moving into an area. Sometimes no enemy turned up; sometimes enemy soldiers were indeed discovered. Either way, the sweep was valuable for ensuring security.

With mission garrisons and prayer partners in place, you now have the means to execute regular sweeps of your marriage and mission to identify possible places of enemy encroachment. In this way you stand a better chance of gaining the upper hand against attack.

Still, while mission garrisons and prayer partners can help with some aspects of performing a sweep, no one knows the intimate details of your marriage like you do. Therefore, each spouse must also participate in searches and sweeps. Part of your marital privilege and responsibility is to cultivate an honest and open dialogue about troublesome areas. As you've been meeting together to read this book, hopefully your level of communication has deepened. Here are some additional suggestions for conducting sweeps and heading off trouble:

- Read and discuss Christian marriage books together.
- Be honest about any temptations and weaknesses you're experiencing, especially those involving friends or colleagues of the opposite sex.
- Exchange phone and Internet passwords, giving each other permission to access online accounts, messaging apps, and social media threads.
- Discuss potentially awkward scenarios. For example, is it acceptable to ride alone in a car or meet for lunch with a person of the opposite sex? Agree in advance on how you will respond to such questions so that you and your spouse are both on the same page.
- Monitor your screen time. Technology can be a huge distraction in marriage. Set up standards such as no cell phone use during meals or conversations.

You don't have to do everything this chapter suggests. Choose the ideas that best fit your marriage. Whatever your marriage mission statement and your marriage mission creed may be, these suggestions will augment, enhance, and fortify them.

It may feel a bit awkward or artificial to engage in some of the conversations and establish the relationships we've suggested in this chapter. Developing authentic transparency with others takes time and prayer. So too a well-guarded marriage. But in the long run, your marriage and God's mission will benefit, and you'll have what it takes to be lifers.

## Pray Together

God, Your Word shows that we're made for relationships. Please provide us with mission garrisons to protect what You're doing and want to do in and through us. May the people You intersect us with be steeped in Your Word and the ways in which You work. May they be filled with Your Holy Spirit and sensitive to what Your Spirit says. We also recognize the need for prayer partners in our lives; please let us know who would be best suited for these roles. Fill these individuals with wisdom, and use them to keep us focused on You and on our marriage. Make us willing to be held accountable, and send garrisons into our lives to be advocates for us. Make us teachable and tender. In Jesus's name. Amen.

## Taking the Next Step

Use these questions as discussion points. You may also wish to record some answers or insights in your journal.

1. Identify individuals or couples who might serve as your mission garrisons. How might you ask for their help?
2. Identify a person who might serve as your prayer partner. As a general rule, husbands should have a male prayer partner and wives should have a female prayer partner. Put together a plan to meet regularly.
3. Look at the suggestions listed on page 198 for conducting a sweep and cultivating honesty in your marriage. Which ones are the most appealing to you and why?
4. Discuss and agree on standards for sharing Internet passwords, monitoring screen time, and meeting with people of the opposite sex. What is okay? What is not okay?

## Chapter 18

# R and R

*Ponder the path of your feet,*
*and let all your ways be established.*

—PROVERBS 4:26 NKJV

If you've been consistently reading this book and discussing the questions, then you've covered a great deal of territory in a relatively short time. You deserve a little R and R: rest and recuperation. In the military, every soldier looked forward to R and R, when we were free to travel outside base camp and get some much-needed rejuvenation.

For the purposes of this chapter, we'll define R and R a little differently than the military does: rest and reassessment.

## TIME TO REST

Rest involves stepping away from your mission and can include things like recreation, vacation, and sleep. Unfortunately, rest is not valued in our fast-paced society. We run from one meeting, game, or engagement to the next. Mobile technology has increased the speed of life and feeds our inability to shut off our brain and body. But God created us with a need for rest. Resting allows us to regroup and renew, to refresh our energy and recharge our vitality.

Perhaps you fear that by resting, you'll leave undone something that needs to be accomplished. But taking time out indicates that you trust God enough to handle it. I (Penny) admit to suffering from I-have-to-do-it-all syndrome. I was raised by a father who highly valued hard work around the clock, and learning how to engage in times of rest will always be a work in progress for me. I am a "first responder" at heart. But I am slowly coming to understand that making myself shut down all screens, demands on my time, and involvement with others allows my mind and body to settle down and rejuvenate.

There are numerous references to rest in the Bible. God Himself rested after creating the world (Gen. 2:2). Joshua, along with all Israel, was given rest from his enemies (Josh. 21:43–44). And Nehemiah went to great lengths to protect the Sabbath rest (Neh. 13:19) in Jerusalem. While many people think of rest as something physical, God also provides for and validates other kinds of rest:

+ *Rest from service or ministry*: "Then, because so many people were coming and going that they did not even have a chance to eat, [Jesus] said to them, 'Come with me by yourselves to a quiet place and get some rest'" (Mark 6:31).
+ *Rest from anxiety and trouble*: "Rest in the LORD, and wait patiently for Him; do not fret because of him who prospers in his way, because of the man who brings wicked schemes to pass" (Ps. 37:7 NKJV).
+ *Rest for the heart*: "This is how we know that we belong to the truth and how we set our hearts at rest in his presence" (1 John 3:19).
+ *Rest for the soul*: "Come to me, all you who are weary and burdened, and I will give you rest. Take my yoke upon you and learn from me, for I am gentle and humble in heart, and you will find rest for your souls. For my yoke is easy and my burden is light" (Matt. 11:28–30).

Sometimes you can meet your spouse's need for rest by serving him or her. Serving your spouse can take many forms, such as massaging his or her feet, hands, or back. Taking over a chore, making a special meal or treat, or taking the kids out for a few hours to give your spouse some alone time are all ways you can serve your spouse's need for rest.

Serve One Another, David and Cindy • *3:02 minutes*

Rest looks different from one person to the next. Your spouse may find reading a magazine restful, while your idea of rest is a good old-fashioned nap on a Sunday afternoon. Whatever works for you is right! You know best what things ease your body, heart, and mind. Whatever they are, engage in them regularly. Resting isn't so much about *how* you rest but simply *that* you rest.

## TIME TO REASSESS

Besides rest, reassessment is also vital to your mission. Reassessment means *regularly setting aside time to evaluate your progress.* Similar to an employee evaluation at work, reflecting on God's mission is a time to measure growth and identify areas that need further development. You could compare it to the 5,000-mile maintenance checks on your vehicle. You don't keep driving without getting the oil changed and the tires rotated. Instead, you stop, make an appointment, and take the car in for service. Most service stations check under the hood and give you a printed report that includes any problem areas and the maintenance that was performed. That's exactly what we're suggesting in relation to God's mission. Stop, set aside some time, evaluate your progress, and make necessary adjustments.

## WHY IS REASSESSMENT IMPORTANT?

Taking time to reflect is a tangible way to recount what God has done. It also provides you with the opportunity to process your experiences, express gratitude, and make changes as needed. Sometimes you can't move forward until you look back at where you've been. Learning from the past can inform future plans, decisions, and choices. It also allows you to more thoroughly do the following:

- Protect the integrity of your mission and your marriage
- Inspect your marriage mission statement and marriage mission creed for areas of compromise
- Assess your relationships and diagnose problem areas
- Repair broken parts
- Improve things that are out of date
- Inspect each of your seven marriage sectors for intentional inverse choices
- Assess your relationships with your prayer partners and mission garrisons
- Thank God for all you've experienced

Another benefit of regular evaluation is that when an unexpected crisis arises, you'll have a better chance of dealing with it as a team instead of caving in to the pressure and pushing against each other. Have you ever watched as the first in a trail of upright dominoes is tipped over? The chain reaction cannot be stopped. That's how many people function today; there's no room for error. Push over that first domino and everything else tumbles. Without time and space set around God's mission, you can't deal as effectively when the unexpected unfolds. Granted, there are times when you're flung into the fire, but at least those flames have less chance of consuming you.

Without regular evaluation, problems will go undetected longer, and the damage takes much more time and effort to repair. Since lack of evaluation is a major contributor to severe marital breakdown, let's park here for a few moments with another illustration from Nehemiah.

Once the repair work on Jerusalem's walls was finished, the Israelites lavishly celebrated as in days of old. Not only had the walls and gates around the city been restored but Nehemiah also instituted various reforms regarding the city's inhabitants and practices in the temple. Afterward, Nehemiah returned to Persia and his service under King Artaxerxes.

Commentators speculate that Nehemiah stayed in Persia for a year or two before returning to Jerusalem to check on the state of the people and the city he so deeply loved (Neh. 13:6–7). Then he discovered a monumental mess.

- Foreign nations were allowed into the assembly of God, which was forbidden under the Law (Neh. 13:1–2).
- The high priest, Eliashib, had converted a sacred room in the temple into living quarters for one of his relatives, Tobiah, an enemy of the Israelites. Years earlier, this man had rallied against Jerusalem's restoration (vv. 4–5).
- The conversion of this sacred room negatively affected worship in the temple since none of the items for worship could be properly stored. Therefore, the Levites who were to serve in the temple left their service because they were not receiving tithes (vv. 5, 10).
- Goods were being sold and traded on the Sabbath—a sacred, holy day and an integral part of God's covenant with His people (vv. 15–18, 20). The Sabbath was thus being desecrated.
- The Israelites reverted back to old behavior patterns and sins that had gotten their ancestors exiled in the first place (v. 18).
- Intermarriage of the Israelites with the pagans of foreign nations

caused the lineage of God's people to be in grave danger of wide-spread illiteracy. How could the children of these mixed marriages ever learn the Hebrew language and read the sacred texts (vv. 23–27)?

What Nehemiah discovered was utterly disconcerting. Things had gotten way out of hand in only a year or two. His hopes to find a reformed community were crushed. Had his years of hard labor been a complete waste? Once again Nehemiah would have to roll up his sleeves to repair what had broken down. According to the Bible, Nehemiah jumped in, rebuking the leaders and the people, commanding those in charge of worship to purify themselves, and calling upon God for both His justice and His favor.

The Bible doesn't say how long it took Nehemiah to repair what had fallen apart over the short time he was away, but it is safe to speculate that regular evaluations could have saved him a lot of time, work, and heartache.

Now that you better understand the need to set aside regular times of reassessment, you will need the tools to effectively conduct an assessment. We share several ideas on the following pages. Some of the tools are less time-consuming than others. We will start with some simple exercises and questions and move to more formal assessment tools. Whichever form(s) of assessment you choose, view the process as another important step on your mission together instead of as an optional exercise. How often should you use the assessment tools? A safe answer is no less than three times a year.

## REASSESSMENT TOOL #1:
## DISCUSSION STARTERS/JOURNAL PROMPTS

Use any or all of the following discussion questions and journal prompts to assess your progress.

- Look back through previous chapters of this book and specifically comment on any positive changes and growth you've noticed in one another and in your marriage.
- Review your marriage mission statement. In what ways do you feel aligned with your mission statement? How might you be deviating from it in attitude or action?
- Review your marriage mission creed. In what tangible ways are you actively adhering to your beliefs? What areas need some added attention?
- If you've been using a journal, flip back through it and read some of your early entries to your spouse. Note any miracles, blessings, or answers to prayer God has given you, and thank Him for those things. Discuss points of struggle and success, and thank God for those too. Record any new reflections in your journal.
- Assess the goals you set for the people, permissions, and provisions needed for your mission. Have you achieved your goals? Are there new goals that need to be set?

Write your responses to the following in your journal.

- Since discovering God's mission for our marriage, the three most interesting revelations I've had about my relationship with God are . . .
- The three most interesting revelations I've had about our marriage are . . .
- The three most interesting revelations I've had about God's mission for our marriage are . . .
- A couple of things that still puzzle me are . . .
- The thing that most surprised me about God's mission is . . .
- If I could ask God three questions about His mission for our marriage, they would be . . .

- The three most positive changes I've noticed in myself are . . .
- The three most positive changes I've noticed in my spouse are . . .
- The areas in which I am still struggling are . . .
- If I could change one thing about our marriage, it would be . . .
- If I could change one thing about God's mission, it would be . . .

## REASSESSMENT TOOL #2:
## RETREAT TO ADVANCE

In our first book, *Marriage on the Mend: Healing Your Relationship After Crisis, Separation, and Divorce,* we wrote about a marriage assessment tool called the Mini Marriage Retreat. Every ninety days Clint and I retreat with God to deepen our relationship with Him, each other, and His mission for our marriage. This retreat basically consists of finding a cheap hotel for two nights, unplugging from technology, reviewing the past quarter of our marriage and mission in all seven sectors, setting goals for the coming quarter, and praying together. As of this writing, we've retreated fifty-eight times. These retreats have allowed for extremely meaningful dialogue, ongoing assessment, and growth.

 Mini Marriage Retreat, Ron and Doris • *7:04 minutes*

 Mini Marriage Retreat, David and Cindy • *4:21 minutes*

The Mini Marriage Retreat originally started out as a way to assess and strengthen our marriage four times a year. Over time it also became a way to assess God's mission for our marriage. Here's a suggested layout for using the Mini Marriage Retreat.

First, decide how often you are going to retreat. Book your hotel accordingly. We suggest staying relatively close to home so that you don't need to spend a lot of time traveling unless that's your thing and it provides you with quiet space. Hotel check-in is usually three o'clock. Check into your room and spend that first night going on a date.

The next morning, spend time with God individually and then take a walk together. Afterward, sit down and review your marriage mission statement, creed, and goals. Look back at the goals you've set in the past and look forward by setting new goals. Use a special pad of paper or journal for these retreats. Pray together over all your goals and plans.

You may choose to review all seven sectors of marriage, as we do, or just stick to assessing God's mission for your marriage. We incorporated the assessment of our mission under the professional sector since it has become our career. Some couples assess their mission under the big dreams sector; some place it under the spiritual sector. Choose what works for you. Take breaks as necessary. When you're done with the assessment, catch a movie, play a game, or do something you enjoy together that doesn't require heavy discussion. Return home the next day.

If you can't afford to do something like this, there are options. Instead of going away to a hotel, take a day off to go to a park or quiet space where you can be alone and uninterrupted for a few hours. Adapt this tool to best fit your needs.

## REASSESSMENT TOOL #3:
## MARRIAGE MISSION RATING SCALE

For those who prefer a more formalized assessment tool, use the following rating scale. Mark your responses on a scale of one through ten and then compare your answers with your spouse. Discuss any areas of discrepancy.

Our marriage mission is focused on the assigned task as stated by our marriage mission statement.

Unfocused                                                    Very focused
1       2       3       4       5       6       7       8       9       10

Our marriage mission is making progress on the goals we set at regular intervals.

No progress                                                  Much progress
1       2       3       4       5       6       7       8       9       10

Our marriage mission is aligned with the Bible in every area of execution.

No alignment                                            Complete alignment
1       2       3       4       5       6       7       8       9       10

Our marriage mission consistently demonstrates God's Law of Inversion.

No demonstration                                    Consistent demonstration
1       2       3       4       5       6       7       8       9       10

We consistently spend time with God each day.

Not at all                                                          Always
1       2       3       4       5       6       7       8       9       10

We consistently share our rations (time, treasure, talent, and testimony) with others through our marriage mission.

No sharing                                                  Always sharing
1       2       3       4       5       6       7       8       9       10

We utilize the mission garrisons God has given us.

Not at all                                                      Always
1        2        3        4        5        6        7        8        9        10

We effectively handle our hardships and do so as a coordinated team.

Not at all                                                      Always
1        2        3        4        5        6        7        8        9        10

We regularly meet with our prayer partners.

Not at all                                                      Always
1        2        3        4        5        6        7        8        9        10

We demonstrate faith according to the beliefs set forth in our marriage mission creed.

Not at all                                                      Always
1        2        3        4        5        6        7        8        9        10

We behave in ways consistent with God's design for marriage: leading and following.

Not at all                                                      Always
1        2        3        4        5        6        7        8        9        10

We carry out our assigned task as a unified team.

Not at all                                                      Always
1        2        3        4        5        6        7        8        9        10

It's not necessary that you use all the tools provided in this chapter. Use the tool(s) that best suits your marriage and mission—or design your own assessment tool. What matters is that you use something to keep you heading in the right direction.

## COMMEMORATE YOUR PROGRESS

Some couples find it meaningful to mark their milestones with something symbolic to represent what God has done, be it a goal accomplished or some other meaningful occurrence. The Bible is full of symbols that serve as reminders of our spiritual lives and God's spiritual truths. The cross of Christ is the most powerful biblical symbol for a Christian, but there are many others. For example, when Joshua and the Israelites crossed the Jordan River, God instructed them to set up a special memorial to remind them of His deliverance: "When the whole nation had finished crossing the Jordan, the LORD said to Joshua, 'Choose twelve men from among the people, one from each tribe, and tell them to take up twelve stones from the middle of the Jordan, from right where the priests are standing, and carry them over with you and put them down at the place where you stay tonight'" (Josh. 4:1–3).

A few verses later, Joshua told the people that the stones were to serve as a sign among them (v. 6). When their children asked about the meaning of the stones, the Israelites were to recall the miracle God performed in that place (v. 7). J. Vernon McGee offers this wisdom on the symbolism behind the memorial: "The twelve stones taken out of the Jordan and put on the west bank of the river were a reminder of God's tremendous power on Israel's behalf."[10]

Symbols represent truth and signify a reminder of something spiritually significant. Before we left for the Holy Land in 2011, a friend sent Clint and me two small pendants in the shape of a shield. Engraved on the back was our theme verse for the mission: "Be strong and courageous. Do not be terrified; do not be discouraged, for the LORD your God will be with you wherever you go" (Josh. 1:9 NIV 1984). Those pendants were a powerful reminder that God was with us at all times. Whenever we look at them, we remember all that He did on our behalf.

Create a marriage memorial to symbolize and commemorate a

particular phase, season, or highlight of your mission. This could be something as simple as a stone that you paint or decorate together. If crafting isn't your thing, look for a pendant or pocket token (available at Christian bookstores) to serve as your symbol. Or frame a verse that has been particularly meaningful to you and hang it in a prominent place in your home.

You and your spouse are doing something together that is extremely unique. Not all couples will attempt to discover God's mission for them. It's hard work! Assessing and commemorating your progress remind you that God is pleased with what you're doing together, and you can be assured that He will honor your labor in unimaginable ways. "Let us not become weary in doing good, for at the proper time we will reap a harvest if we do not give up" (Gal. 6:9).

## Pray Together

God, please help us measure our lives, our marriage, and Your mission with Your eyes, not our own. We need Your holy vision and assessment to become the people You want us to be. Father God, show us how to be humble and serve one another. We realize that R and R is important. Show us what this looks like for our marriage and mission. How can we best assess what You have called us to do and keep ourselves in alignment with Your desires? By Your Spirit, please guide us in measuring progress and moving forward. In Jesus's name. Amen.

## Taking the Next Step

Use these questions as discussion points. You may also wish to record some answers or insights in your journal.

1. In your own words, explain why regular rest and reassessment are necessary.

2. What are some tangible ways that you rest (napping, reading, getting outdoors, etc.)?

3. Which types of assessment tools most interest you: informal (like the discussion prompts on pages 207–208) or formal (like the rating scale on pages 210–211)? Why?

4. Is it feasible for you to schedule a Mini Marriage Retreat based on the ideas from this chapter? Why or why not?

5. Set a date for your next reassessment and decide which tool(s) you will use.

# Chapter 19

# Forward, March!

*I will not follow where the path may lead, but I will*
*go where there is no path, and I will leave a trail.*
—MURIEL STRODE, "Wind-Wafted Wild Flowers"

You are nearing the end of *Your Marriage, God's Mission*. We trust God has moved in your lives as you've been seeking Him, because you've been in His Word and in prayer together. And God always moves when His people draw near: "Draw near to God and He will draw near to you" (James 4:8 NKJV).

As we round this final turn, picture yourselves as Israelites under Joshua's leadership, now standing well within the Promised Land. Mission accomplished. Close your eyes and imagine what you might have seen, smelled, tasted, touched, and heard standing in the middle of this rich, God-given territory of unlimited possibility. No doubt the Israelites were joyous in this new place. With much bloodshed they had driven out enemy nations and fought hard to possess it. Now they could live out the rest of their lives in a land of increase and fruitfulness: "Hear, Israel, and be careful to obey so that it may go well with you and that you may increase greatly in a land flowing with milk and honey, just as the LORD, the God of your ancestors, promised you" (Deut. 6:3).

Clint and I have seen the land of Israel, and it is extraordinary. Driving through the countryside, we passed long stretches of fertile farmlands overflowing with grain and produce. The land is sacred in every way.

Having said that, we pose a question that may seem a bit . . . odd. What if the Promised Land had been one big, fat disappointment for the Israelites? What if, given all the Pharaoh fleeing, enemy confronting, battle waging, life losing, and faith leaping behind them, the Promised Land wasn't very promising after all? What then? Would the Israelites have revolted in anger and dismay? Would God's people have raised their fists and grumbled against Him again? Would one glance at their sparse surroundings have set in motion the familiar cycle of apostasy?

Given the human condition, it would be safe to speculate that that is exactly what would have happened. Actually, it did. Not that the Promised Land turned out to be a bust or a bummer, but as time passed, the people turned their hearts away from God yet again.

To no avail, Joshua went to great efforts right up to the end of his life to remind God's people of His faithfulness and His requirements for living in the Promised Land.

Now I am about to go the way of all the earth. You know with all your heart and soul that not one of all the good promises the LORD your God gave you has failed. Every promise has been fulfilled; not one has failed. But just as all the good things the LORD your God has promised you have come to you, so he will bring on you all the evil things he has threatened, until the LORD your God has destroyed you from this good land he has given you. If you violate the covenant of the LORD your God, which he commanded you, and go and serve other gods and bow down to them, the LORD's anger will burn against you, and you will

quickly perish from the good land he has given you. (Josh.
23:14–16)

Joshua's warning had good cause. Israel had amply demonstrated
their disobedience during their flight from Egypt, and God punished them accordingly. The distance between Egypt and the
Promised Land was only a little more than two hundred miles, yet
the Israelites were caught in a revolving door of desert wandering
for forty years because they resisted God's ways. And their attitude
didn't change once they completed their mission to get from Egypt
to the Promised Land. Despite Joshua's admonition, the Israelites
wandered away from God many times. They forsook everything He
had spoken about their future in exchange for what they could grab
hold of in the present. Chronic rebellion fills many pages of the Old
Testament. Why? God alone knows, but it is safe to speculate that
His people suffered from a spiritual disease wound into their DNA
since the fall. They were severely shortsighted.

## BACKWARD DESIGN

God created the beginning of all things with the end of all things in
full view. God always begins a work with the end in mind. He penned
the first page of His Word with the ink on the last page already dry.

Think about Jesus. He knew His earthly life would end at Calvary,
and He lived accordingly. Jesus knew His death on the cross would
mean He'd live a blameless, sinless life every single day until He
hung there. And that's exactly the life He lived.

Although we would never attempt to compare our thinking with
God's, we have tried our best to write *Your Marriage, God's Mission*
with a similar backward design. While we weren't sure about what
we'd write on every page, our hope was that by the end of the book,
your faith would be radically impacted. Because when all is said and
done, that's what matters most.

Now it's your turn. Think about the finish line of your journey together. What would you want God to say about your marriage and His mission when you join Him in heaven? What would you want God to say about you and your time on earth?

Often referred to as the "faith chapter," Hebrews 11 confirms that the Bible's heroes of old were commended for their faith, not their missions (vv. 2, 39). They started with faith and ended with faith, and their missions were sandwiched *in between*. And so it will be for you as well: God's mission is secondary to your faith in God.

Maybe you still feel unsure about what God's mission is for your marriage. Don't be discouraged! Exercise the faith to believe that He will clarify your mission in His time. This season of uncertainty is when your faith must raise its hackles and come bounding in. One day Jesus will ride in on His white horse and save the day, but until then it is your faith that must stand tall. Today. Now.

Wherever you find yourself with regard to carrying out God's mission, Clint and I believe He is doing a mighty work of faith in you and that He will do a mighty work of faith through you. Although you've come to the end of this book, we believe God is just getting started. We hope you believe that too. Therefore, before we part ways, receive these final charges as high-octane fuel in your tank and artillery in your arsenal.

## YOU ARE CHARGED TO BLESS GOD

In the Bible, the Hebrew word most frequently translated "bless" comes from the word *barak*, which means to declare or petition God for beneficial things on someone else's behalf. In most churches and Christian circles today, the words *bless* and *blessing* often denote something good a person receives. For example, someone might say, "I received a blessing in the mail today" to describe an encouraging letter from a friend or maybe an unexpected check.

However, in biblical times when the Jews spoke of blessing, they referred to the Hebrew custom of blessing *God* first and foremost. This is especially manifested in the Psalms: "Let the whole world bless our God and loudly sing his praises" (Psalm 66:8 NLT).

Your mission, first and foremost, should bless God before it blesses man. This is your highest aim. God has entrusted you with this mission; worship Him with it. In *Bless You,* John D. Garr writes, "By focusing man's attention on the God who is good, the ongoing experience of blessing maintains a distinct God-consciousness in the soul and makes every moment of the day a sacred experience."[11] In the Old Testament, the Hebrew word translated *bless* literally means "to kneel." This indicates a holy posture before God. Be concerned with blessing God as your first response to Him each day.

The possibilities for worshipping or blessing God are limitless. One simple idea is to praise Him through gratitude statements such as these:

I bless You, God.
You alone are holy.
I bless You for Your unlimited power.
You alone are righteous.
I bless You with my words and deeds.
You alone are omnipotent.
I bless You with my voice.
You alone are just and true.

Blessing God means adoring Him for His attributes. Perhaps you begin each day with the words from Psalm 103:1, "Bless the LORD, O my soul; and all that is within me, bless His holy name" (NKJV).

Blessing God means honoring Him with acts of worship with your body, heart, soul, and mind. Garr writes, "Blessing God is an exercise of the whole person, both a mental and a visceral action that is exercised every day, and even then, it is not just a once-a-day exercise. . . . When Christians come to recognize the rich Hebraic blessing heritage that was foundational to the faith of Jesus and the apostles, they too will 'bless the Lord at all times' and will find themselves 'giving thanks' in all things."[12]

## YOU ARE CHARGED TO BRING CHANGE

The first blessing God bestowed on man was given to a married couple, Adam and Eve, as He sent them off on His mission. "God blessed them and said to them, 'Be fruitful and increase in number; fill the earth and subdue it. Rule over the fish in the sea and the birds in the sky and over every living creature that moves on the ground'" (Gen. 1:28). Adam and Eve were charged to bring about change. Actually, every person to whom God assigned a task was charged to leave a mark of transformation in the lives of those they were sent to serve. God's missions were intended to bring about changes in the human heart.

In Jesus's final words to His disciples before ascending to heaven, He charged them to be ambassadors of change in the lives of others. "Go therefore and make disciples of all the nations, baptizing them in the name of the Father and of the Son and of the Holy Spirit" (Matt. 28:19 NKJV).

Through God's mission for your marriage, you've also been charged with the responsibility to bring about change in someone else's life. God creates the change, but you are His conduit to deliver it. Think about that truth for a moment. Out of every couple God could have chosen for the assigned task at hand, He chose you. This is your mission. This is your time. Go, therefore, and change what needs to be changed.

## YOU ARE CHARGED TO BE CHANGED

God rewards and blesses those who follow His commands. In other words, as you carry out His assigned task, not only will other people be changed, but you will change too. How do we know? The Bible says God will make positive changes in the lives of those who do the following:

- Diligently seek Him (Heb. 11:6).
- Do not give up (Gal. 6:9).
- Help others in need, especially the poor (Ps. 41:1–2).
- Practice generosity and lend freely (Ps. 37:26).
- Fear God and take refuge in Him (Ps. 31:19).
- Hear God's Word and put it into practice (Luke 11:28).
- Suffer for doing what is right (1 Peter 3:14).
- Bring God a tithe (Mal. 3:10).
- Find wisdom and gain understanding (Prov. 3:13).
- Believe in Him even though He is unseen (John 20:29).
- Persevere under trial (James 1:12).
- Constantly do what is right (Ps. 106:3).

That list of promises and blessings contains many of the concepts you've read about in this book, such as following God's OPORDs, making inverse choices, exercising plan faith, sharing your rations, and suffering inside of His will. Your mission will bring about change and your mission will change you—all for the good and the glory of God.

## YOU ARE CHARGED TO BLESS OTHERS

In addition to blessing God, you have the privilege of bestowing happiness and prosperity both on your spouse and on other people outside your marriage. Bestowing these blessings simply means giving something to someone or providing a beneficial service to others.

Bestowing a blessing may also take the form of actually invoking God to place His blessing on someone. In ancient times, it was the priests' responsibility to invoke blessing. But God's Word says you are a priest (Rev. 5:10). Therefore you have the privilege of speaking blessing over others because God has blessed you. "Praise be to the God and Father of our Lord Jesus Christ, who has blessed us in the heavenly realms with every spiritual blessing in Christ" (Eph. 1:3). You are charged with the God-given responsibility to bless others as you carry out God's mission.

What does it look like to pronounce a blessing on someone in a priestly manner? Two weeks before I (Clint) turned twenty-four, my grandfather, a messianic Jew, called me to his side. Although I didn't fully understand what he was doing at the time, I now know that he was invoking God's blessing upon me. Placing his hands on my body, he simply asked God to bless and reward my life. Although I attended church as a kid, I'd never professed faith in Christ. Now, as a Christian, I am fully convinced of the eternal importance those moments held as I stood before my grandfather. He died two weeks later, on my twenty-fourth birthday.

The night before Penny and I left on our very first forty-day marriage mission, our friends Chuck and Micki Ann came over to our house and spoke a blessing over us. There was no fancy ceremony, just two friends gathering with us in our living room, asking God to bless us, protect us, empower us, and stamp us with His Holy Spirit.

In the same way that my grandfather blessed me and our friends blessed Penny and me, you are charged to impart spoken blessings to others. Think of such a blessing as a biblical statement that asks good things from God on behalf of someone else. A spoken blessing doesn't have to be complicated. The Bible contains many examples. In the Old Testament, the patriarchs Abraham, Isaac, and Jacob all gave formal blessings to their children. In Jacob's case, the blessing was extended to some grandchildren as well. Joshua blessed the Israelites when they took possession of the Promised Land. And in the New Testament, Jesus placed His hands on children and blessed them.

Most blessings include appropriately placing your hands on a person's head, shoulders, or arms and asking God to do good things for him or her. You may also choose to symbolically anoint that person's head, hands, or feet with oil when you bless them. In your own words, a blessing may sound something like this:

> May God protect you and watch over you at all times. May He grant you favor and all that you need to live out His will. May God be gracious to you, fill you with His peace, grant you the desires of your heart, and fill you anew with His Holy Spirit. In the name of the Father, Son, and Holy Spirit, I bless you. Amen.

If you're still not sure what to say, use the priestly (or Aaronic) blessing from the Bible: "The LORD bless you and keep you; the LORD make his face shine on you and be gracious to you; the LORD turn his face toward you and give you peace" (Num. 6:24–26).

Make it a point to get comfortable giving other people a spoken blessing. If you're just learning how, or you feel nervous, then write the blessing down on paper and read it in the person's presence. Practice on your spouse. Practice on your children. Practice blessings count too!

## YOU ARE CHARGED TO BE VICTORIOUS

In the army, every GI in my bunk house had a countdown calendar to mark off the number of days left until they would be rotated out of war zone combat. God has a countdown calendar too. He alone knows the number of days left before the return of Jesus Christ. God also knows the number of your days here, and He wants you to make the most of them. Whatever the length of time until Jesus returns, or however long your own life may be, God has charged you to be victorious: "Thanks be to God! He gives us the victory through our

Lord Jesus Christ. Therefore, my dear brothers and sisters, stand firm. Let nothing move you. Always give yourselves fully to the work of the Lord, because you know that your labor in the Lord is not in vain" (1 Cor. 15:57–58).

Though our world feels so very uncertain, God is firm and unshakeable. He is sure about His purposes. He is sure about you. And He is sure about your mission and your victory. That is why you can rest when all around you feels so very restless. No ifs, ands, or buts. Go raid the enemy's camp! It's a done deal. Satan has been bagged and tagged. God's got this! And God has given you this:

> I will give you every place where you set your foot, as I promised Moses. Your territory will extend from the desert to Lebanon, and from the great river, the Euphrates—all the Hittite country—to the Mediterranean Sea in the west. No one will be able to stand against you all the days of your life. As I was with Moses, so I will be with you; I will never leave you nor forsake you. Be strong and courageous, because you will lead these people to inherit the land I swore to their ancestors to give them. (Josh. 1:3–6)

"Every place where you set your foot" means exactly what it says: *every* place—the mountains high and the valleys low. The barren wilderness and the fertile pastures. The north, south, east, and west. All are yours for the taking.

Though our world is heating up and shaking down all around us, this is only a foretaste of what is to come. Anything we've built our lives upon other than what matters to God will tumble. The only things that will remain are the kingdom of God and the people of God. And although you won't possess your spiritual inheritance without a fight, you have something the Israelites did not have: the cross of Christ. The cross has reconciled the extremes of trouble and triumph. Christ's finished work has given you all that you need to march forward. As you do, the soles of your feet crush the heads of all your enemies. Every single one.

You see, despite the tumultuous state of our world, there is today a Promised Land for the people of God, a land flowing with milk and honey. It is God's gift to His people. But your Promised Land isn't about finding the ultimate destination or achieving some grandiose life goals. It isn't about your marriage or discovering God's mission. The gift we speak of has nothing to do with pleasure, paradise, purpose, or any other created thing. The gift of God's mission is God Himself. Jesus Christ. He is your Promised Land.

"Travel in peace. The mission that you're to accomplish is from the LORD" (Judg. 18:6 ISV).

---

## Pray Together

Heavenly Father, as we come to the end of this portion of our journey, we recognize that You're just getting started. We bless You, God. May the choices we make today facilitate change for tomorrow. Teach us to number our days and realize their brevity so that we do and say what matters most.

Let us engage in Your mission with the end in mind. In light of what awaits us when we cross the finish line and enter heaven's gates, what do You desire for our spiritual lives? Our relationships? Finances? Health? Professions? Home? Big dreams? You are the only One who can help us live in the present with the future in mind. Use Your Word and Your Holy Spirit to start from the end and work backward. No matter what we face, we believe and declare that You are the greatest gift we can ever receive. May we unwrap this gift each day, partaking of Your presence. May we share this gift with others we meet, and impact generations for Your kingdom. May we faithfully take up the charges You have given us to bless You, to bring change and to be changed, to bless each other and others as well, and to live in the full assurance of Your victory. In Jesus's name. Amen.

---

## Taking the Next Step

Use these questions as discussion points. You may also wish to record some answers or insights in your journal.

1.  Resubmit each of the seven sectors of your marriage to God. Ask for His blessing.
2.  Turn back to the thoughts and ideas you wrote down in chapter 3, when we asked whether or not you knew anything about God's mission for your marriage. Are things cloudier or clearer now?
3.  Has anyone ever spoken a blessing over you? If so, what was the circumstance and how did it make you feel?
4.  Write out a blessing that you will speak over your spouse in the coming days. Set aside a special time to bless each other.

# Appendix A
## Resources for Recovery

## BOOKS

Bodishbaugh, Signa. *The Journey to Wholeness in Christ: A Devotional Adventure to Becoming Whole*. Mobile, AL: Journey Press, 1997.

Bodishbaugh, Signa, and Conlee Bodishbaugh. *Illusions of Intimacy: Unmasking Patterns of Sexual Addiction and Bringing Deep Healing to Those Who Struggle*. Tonbridge, England: Sovereign World, 2004.

Gunter, Sylvia. *Prayer Essentials for Living in His Presence*, vol. 1. Birmingham, AL: The Father's Business, 2000.

Rodgers, Beverly, and Tom Rodgers. *Becoming a Family That Heals: How to Resolve Past Issues and Free Your Future*. Carol Stream, IL: Tyndale, 2009.

Stanford, Matthew S. *Grace for the Afflicted: A Clinical and Biblical Perspective on Mental Illness*. Downers Grove, IL: InterVarsity Press, 2008.

## ORGANIZATIONS

Christian Healing Ministries (https://www.christianhealingmin.org/)
>    Francis and Judith MacNutt
>    *Healing prayer and resources for recovery*

Faithful and True Ministries (http://904true.org)
>    Jerry and Susan Sinclair
>    *Recovery from sexual addiction for men and their wives*
>    Hotline: (904) 443-0246

Hope for Mental Health (http://hope4mentalhealth.com)
  Rick and Kay Warren
  *Providing transforming love, support, and hope through the local church*

The Journey to Wholeness in Christ (http://jtwic.org)
  Conlee and Signa Bodishbaugh
  *Twelve-week study by Conlee and Signa Bodishbaugh*

# Appendix B
## Resources for Recovering from Loss

## BOOKS

Bragg, Penny A. *For Those Who Weep: A Grief Response Journal.* Enumclaw, WA: Redemption Press, 2014.

Kent, Carol. *When I Lay My Isaac Down: Unshakable Faith in Unthinkable Circumstances.* Rev. ed. Colorado Springs: NavPress, 2013.

Sittser, Jerry. *A Grace Disguised: How the Soul Grows through Loss.* Grand Rapids: Zondervan, 2004.

Tchividjian, Tullian. *Glorious Ruin: How Suffering Sets You Free.* Colorado Springs: David C. Cook, 2003.

Wright, H. Norman. *Recovering from Losses in Life.* Grand Rapids: Revell, 2006.

Zahnd, Brian. *What to Do on the Worst Day of Your Life.* Lake Mary, FL: Christian Life, 2009.

## ORGANIZATIONS

American Foundation for Suicide Prevention (https://afsp.org)
> *A nonprofit organization that provides resources for suicide prevention and offers healing for loved ones after a death by suicide*

GriefShare (https://www.griefshare.org)
> *A bereavement ministry offering participants a safe place to grieve a loss in a small-group setting*

National Alliance on Mental Illness (https://www.nami.org)
> *A national network to help anyone impacted by mental illness*

# Notes

1. Dave Lind and Dawn Lind, *Have You Made the Inspiring Discovery of a Team of Two Life?* (Rutland, VT: Focus on Purpose, 2011), 3–5.

2. Tommy Tenney, *Prayers of a God Chaser: Passionate Prayers of Pursuit* (Minneapolis: Bethany House, 2002), 151.

3. Dwight D. Eisenhower, "Quotes," Dwight D. Eisenhower Presidential Library, Museum, and Boyhood Home, accessed July 11, 2017, https://www.eisenhower.archives.gov/all_about_ike /quotes.html.

4. Sun Tzu, *The Art of War*, trans. Lionel Giles, The Internet Classics Archive, accessed July 11, 2017, http://classics.mit.edu /Tzu/artwar.html.

5. J. Vernon McGee, *Thru the Bible*, vol. 5, *1 Corinthians through Revelation* (Nashville: Nelson, 1983), 138.

6. Robert Jeffress, *The Solomon Secrets: 10 Keys to Extraordinary Success from Proverbs* (Colorado Springs: WaterBrook Press, 2002), 184–85.

7. Bob Sorge, *The Fire of Delayed Answers: Are You Waiting for Your Prayers to Be Answered?* (Greenwood, MO: Oasis House, 1996), 94.

8. E. M. Bounds, *E. M. Bounds: The Classic Collection on Prayer* (Alachua, FL: Bridge-Logos, 2001), 131.

9. Edwin Hubbell Chapin, quoted in L. B. Cowman, *Streams in the Desert* (Grand Rapids: Zondervan, 1997), 375.

10. J. Vernon McGee, *Thru the Bible*, vol. 2, *Joshua through Psalms* (Nashville: Nelson, 1983), 10.

11. John D. Garr, *Bless You: Restoring the Biblically Hebraic Blessing* (Atlanta: Golden Key Books, 2012), 79–80.

12. Ibid., 85–86.

Also by Clint and Penny A. Bragg

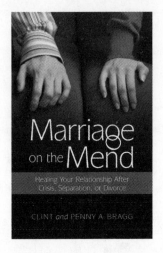

Clint and Penny Bragg's reconciliation after an eleven-year divorce and a three-thousand–mile coast-to-coast separation is nothing short of a modern-day miracle. Through the work of Inverse Ministries, their nonprofit organization, they serve as marriage missionaries: sharing their testimony with audiences, teaching seminars, leading retreats for couples, and equipping ministry leaders across the nation and abroad. Prior to forming Inverse Ministries, Clint and Penny worked as educators in the public school system for a combined total of over twenty years. Their story of reconciliation has been featured on local and national television and radio programs. Originally from the San Francisco Bay Area, Clint and Penny now reside in Arizona. Clint is an avid videographer who plans to make their testimony into a feature film. He also leads husbands' discipleship groups in their community. Penny facilitates classes for those who are grieving and is passionate about writing and creating mixed-media artwork to express her faith and honor God.

To learn more about Inverse Ministries or to invite Clint and Penny to speak at your event, visit InverseMinistries.org.